APOCALYPTIC THEOPOLITICS

THEOPOLITICAL VISIONS

SERIES EDITORS:

Thomas Heilke
D. Stephen Long
and Debra Dean Murphy

Theopolitical Visions seeks to open up new vistas on public life, hosting fresh conversations between theology and political theory. This series assembles writers who wish to revive theopolitical imagination for the sake of our common good.

Theopolitical Visions hopes to re-source modern imaginations with those ancient traditions in which political theorists were often also theologians. Whether it was Jeremiah's prophetic vision of exiles "seeking the peace of the city," Plato's illuminations on piety and the civic virtues in the Republic, St. Paul's call to "a common life worthy of the Gospel," St. Augustine's beatific vision of the City of God, or the gothic heights of medieval political theology, much of Western thought has found it necessary to think theologically about politics, and to think politically about theology. This series is founded in the hope that the renewal of such mutual illumination might make a genuine contribution to the peace of our cities.

FORTHCOMING VOLUMES:

David Deane
The Matter of the Spirit: How Soteriology Shapes the Moral Life

Adam Joyce
No More Pharoahs: Christianity, Racial Capitalism, and Socialism

Apocalyptic
THEOPOLITICS

Essays and Sermons on Eschatology, Ethics, and Politics

ELIZABETH PHILLIPS

CASCADE *Books* · Eugene, Oregon

APOCALYPTIC THEOPOLITICS
Essays and Sermons on Eschatology, Ethics, and Politics

Copyright © 2022 Elizabeth Phillips. All rights reserved. Except for brief quotations in critical publications or reviews, no part of this book may be reproduced in any manner without prior written permission from the publisher. Write: Permissions, Wipf and Stock Publishers, 199 W. 8th Ave., Suite 3, Eugene, OR 97401.

Cascade Books
An Imprint of Wipf and Stock Publishers
199 W. 8th Ave., Suite 3
Eugene, OR 97401

www.wipfandstock.com

PAPERBACK ISBN: 978-1-7252-9027-3
HARDCOVER ISBN: 978-1-7252-9026-6
EBOOK ISBN: 978-1-7252-9028-0

Cataloguing-in-Publication data:

Names: Phillips, Elizabeth, 1973–, author.

Title: Apocalyptic theopolitics : essays and sermons on eschatology, ethics, and politics / Elizabeth Phillips.

Description: Eugene, OR: Cascade Books, 2022 | Series: Theopolitical Visions 28 | Includes bibliographical references.

Identifiers: ISBN 978-1-7252-9027-3 (paperback) | ISBN 978-1-7252-9026-6 (hardcover) | ISBN 978-1-7252-9028-0 (ebook)

Subjects: LCSH: Christianity and politics. | Political theology. | Christian ethics.

Classification: BR115.P7 P479 2022 (print) | BR115.P7 P479 (ebook)

"Eschatology and Political Theology" was originally published as "Eschatology and Apocalyptic," in *The Cambridge Companion to Christian Political Theology*, edited by Craig Hovey and Elizabeth Phillips, 274–96 (Cambridge: Cambridge University Press, 2015). Reprinted by permission of the publisher.

"Political Theology and Theological Ethics" was originally published as "Politics and Political Theology," in *The T&T Clark Handbook of Christian Ethics*, edited by Tobias Winright, 155–63 (London: T&T Clark, 2021). Reprinted by permission of the publisher.

"Future Hope/Present Realities: A Sermon on the Life and Work of James Cone," originally preached as "James Cone," Trinity College Chapel, Cambridge, England, April 24, 2016.

"A Surprising and Mysterious Unity: A Pentecost Sermon" was originally preached (untitled) at Westcott House, Cambridge, England, May 18, 2021.

"Charting the 'Ethnographic Turn'" was originally published as "Charting the 'Ethnographic Turn': Theologians and the Study of Christian Congregations," in *Perspectives on Ecclesiology and Ethnography*, edited by Pete Ward, 95–106 (Grand Rapids: Eerdmans, 2012). Reprinted by permission of the publisher.

"Saying 'Peace' When There Is No Peace: An American Christian Zionist Congregation on Peace, Militarism and Settlements" was originally published in *Comprehending Christian Zionism: Perspectives in Comparison*, edited by Göran Gunner and Robert Smith, 15–32 (Minneapolis: Fortress, 2014). Reprinted by permission of the publisher.

"Against Anxiety, Beyond Triumphalism: An Eastertide Sermon" was originally preached as "Against Anxiety, Beyond Triumphalism," Clare College Chapel, Cambridge, England, May 17, 2009.

"'We've Read the End of the Book': An Engagement with Contemporary Christian Zionism through the Eschatology of John Howard Yoder" was originally published in *Studies in Christian Ethics* 21, no. 3 (2008) 342–61. Reprinted by permission of the publisher.

"Doctrines of 'The Two': The Church and the Elusive 'Public' in Augustine and Yoder" was originally published as "The Church and the Elusive 'Public,'" in *Grace, Governance and Globalization: Theology and Public Life*, edited by Lieven Boeve et al., 238–47 (London: T&T Clark, 2017).

"Heroes/Villains: Anabaptism and the Rise and Fall of Yoder in Political Theology" was originally published as "Anabaptist Theologies," in *The Blackwell Companion to Political Theology*, edited by Peter Scott and William Cavanaugh, 333–46, 2nd ed. (Oxford: Wiley-Blackwell, 2019). Reprinted by permission of the publisher.

"Sixteenth-Century Theopolitics: A Sermon for the 500th Anniversary of the Reformation" was originally preached as "Reformation Theopolitics," St. John's College Chapel, Cambridge, England, October 22, 2017.

"Narrating Catastrophe, Cultivating Hope: Apocalyptic Practices and Theological Virtue" was originally published in *Studies in Christian Ethics* 31, no. 1 (February 1, 2018) 17–33. Reprinted by permission of the publisher.

"Glimpses: A Sermon in Preparation for Lent" was originally preached as "Glimpses of Heaven," Westcott House, Cambridge, England, February 12, 2015.

"Penetrating the Surface of Reality: A Sermon on Flannery O'Conner for All Hallows' Eve" was originally preached as "Flannery O'Connor," King's College Chapel, Cambridge, England, October 30, 2016.

For my brother,
David Hall (1971–2019)
One of the many unknown and unsung saintly souls that are crushed
by the weight of the brokenness of this world as they dedicate their
lives to mending it for the sake of others.

Contents

Acknowledgments

I gratefully acknowledge all those involved in the original delivery and publication of the sermons and essays included in this collection. I am grateful to my colleagues and students at Westcott House, to the Cambridge college deans and chaplains who invited me to preach in their chapels, and to the publishers of journals and books who gave their permission for republication in this format.

Introduction

This book brings together a selection of academic pieces and a selection of sermons, all chosen for their shared work at the intersections of eschatology, ethics, and politics. Only minimal editing has been done for this collection, so that the pieces largely appear just as they were originally published or delivered; shifts in my thinking and writing should be as evident as the recurring similarities throughout.

The selections are organized into three parts. Part I, "Ends and the End," highlights intersections between the two main disciplines in which I have worked (Christian ethics and political theology) and the prominence of the theme of eschatology in my ways of engaging in both fields. Part II, "Ethnography of Eschatology," arises from my ethnographic work on American Christian Zionism.

Part III, "Eschatology and Nonviolent Witness," shows the depth to which my work has been influenced by Anabaptism in general, and the work of John Howard Yoder in particular, as well as a journey of gaining necessary critical distance from Yoder during the years when I and many others learned the truth of his personal legacy. I now find Yoder's work mostly unusable, though I know that its mark on my theology will never disappear. I do not want it to disappear insofar as his work was my initiation into all that is best in Anabaptism and to the transformative power of nonviolence. I hope that it continues to fade away insofar as it was not only insufficient (as all our theological work is), but also instantiated the same impulses and systems which allowed him to abuse and assault women for most of his adult life.

Part IV, "Apocalyptic," hones in on a theme which is already evident in previous sections: the normative use of apocalyptic in ethics and politics.

This section focuses on how apocalyptic as a genre narrates violence and suffering, but for the purposes of hope and resistance.

In each of these sections, pieces which were originally published as peer reviewed journal articles or book chapters are followed by sermons which pick up themes from this academic work and reshape it for homiletic purposes. Gathered as a collection, which therefore does not have a single sustained argument, I nonetheless hope that in addition to the arguments made in each piece, this volume overall:

- *argues for interdisciplinarity.* I work at the intersections of Christian ethics, political theology, and ethnography with attention to doctrine, Bible, and critical perspectives. Although none of us can specialize in so many areas with any consistent depth of expertise, we should nonetheless swallow our disciplinary pride and reach out across boundaries created by the ever-growing breadth of knowledge and proliferation of specialisms in the modern academy. Although I know many in the academy believe that work is diluted by breadth of engagement beyond specialization, I believe we are impoverished when we do not learn from one another.

- *argues for keeping traditional sources and contemporary critical perspectives in conversation with one another.* The divisions between our disciplines have some positive purpose, allowing for depth of enquiry through specialization. But the divisions that police a separation between work which engages traditional sources as authoritative on the one hand, and work which attends to contemporary and critical theories on the other hand, seem to me to lack positive purpose and contribute only to impoverishment. When I encounter theology that attends closely to sources like Augustine and Aquinas, but proceeds as if critical, contextual, and liberative perspectives are irrelevant or distracting, I despair. When I encounter theology that attends closely to contemporary experience and critical analysis, but proceeds as if no one had anything valuable to say about this world, its politics, or God before the late-twentieth century, I despair. When I encounter work that puts traditional/historical and critical/liberative sources and approaches into meaningful conversation with one another, then I get interested. I would say that the earliest work in this collection does not enact this commitment as well as I hope the more recent work does.

Both my resolve in this regard and my breadth of engagement have grown, and need to grow much further still.

• *argues for preaching ethics and politics in ways that are not so didactic or partisan to be alienating, but also not so anodyne and unthreatening as to be without challenge.* It is important to acknowledge that the sermons in this volume will not likely translate directly into preachability in other contexts. I have been preaching in a very strange little world. The University of Cambridge is made up of thirty-one colleges, and most of these colleges have their own chapels where very small numbers of people pray daily and very slightly larger numbers of people gather weekly (during the academic terms) for services which are attended more for the beauty of their choral tradition than for the preaching. Nearly everyone attending these services is currently studying, teaching, or researching in the University of Cambridge. (To some, this description will sound like a magical world which reminds them of books and films they have loved and would love to enter; to others, it will sound like ensconcement within the worst kind of elitist bastion of a world they would like to dismantle. As an American who has studied and worked in Cambridge for over seventeen years, I would say that I still feel a decent degree of both those reactions.) All these sermons were preached in one of these college chapels, or for my students and colleagues in the Anglican theological college where I worked for over a decade. Yet although these may not be average Sunday sermons, I hope they still communicate something of the importance of preaching ethics and politics, and doing so in ways which challenge without inspiring guilt, inform without being overly didactic, and express a point of view without being partisan. Preaching is *gospel* preaching when it intersects with our common life, when it searches us, when it demands something of us, and when it opens up possibilities for how to respond to God anew.

I. Ends and the End:
Eschatology, Ethics, and Political Theology

CHAPTER 1

Eschatology and Political Theology (2015)

Christian political theology has always been eschatological. This statement may come as a surprise to the casual theologian or politician who is likely to find the connection between eschatology and politics either irrelevant or potentially dangerous. Surely beliefs related to the return of Jesus to earth at the end of time, and the afterlife that follows, either have nothing to do with contemporary politics or could only have harmful influence in the political arena? Memories arise from Christian history of apocalyptic revolutionaries whose theopolitical movements punctuate the middle and early modern ages like flash paper, burning hot and bright but ever so briefly. Are not these the sorts of Christians for whom eschatology, and particularly apocalyptic, is politically normative? In fact, we find that from the Bible to Augustine to Aquinas to the beginnings of the academic discipline called "political theology," theological texts about politics have nearly always been saturated with eschatology and apocalyptic.

My exploration of eschatology and apocalyptic in political theology will proceed in three parts. Part 1 describes the centrality of eschatology in both the traditional sources and twentieth-century emergence of the discipline of political theology. Part 2 considers the eschatologies of nineteenth- and twentieth-century Protestantism in the North Atlantic, a context of great ferment in relation to the eschatological concepts of the millennium and the kingdom of God. Part 3 takes these two discussions into account and asks how apocalyptic can function normatively in contemporary political theologies as it did within the canon of Scripture.

ESCHATOLOGY IN TEXTS AND TRADITIONS OF POLITICAL THEOLOGY

Eschatology and Politics in Scripture

In the Jewish and Christian Scriptures, eschatology and politics are unmistakably interwoven. Although convictions about the end of the world and the afterlife do not seem to have entered into Jewish thought until the Maccabean period, and only the first hints of such beliefs can be seen in canonical books outside the Apocrypha, eschatology is not absent from the Hebrew Scriptures. Within the prophetic books (and perhaps also some Psalms) there are both apocalyptic texts and nonapocalyptic eschatological texts where we find messages of a coming age in which God will act decisively to transform human society and all of creation.

In the popular imagination of many Christians, all biblical eschatology is related to otherworldly realities and is marked by the judgment of individuals; Jewish eschatology is thought to share these themes and also to be marked by the expectation of a coming messiah. In reality, for most of ancient Israel's history, prophetic eschatology was decidedly this-worldly and had very little to do with the fate of individuals or a messianic figure. Instead, these were visions of a coming messianic age in which the kingdoms of the world will be judged, peace and justice will be established, and human society will be transformed. During this age, God will act to gather the people of Israel (in some texts, this includes a focus on Mount Zion and the Temple being rebuilt), judge Israel's enemies, and extend the blessings of Israel to the nations; all creation will be renewed, the people will be truly faithful to God, and nature will be fruitful and cooperative; and there will be no violence, either between people or other animals. Many of these themes come together in the following passage from Zechariah 8:

> Thus says the Lord: I will return to Zion, and will dwell in the midst of Jerusalem; Jerusalem shall be called the faithful city, and the mountain of the Lord of hosts shall be called the holy mountain . . . Thus says the Lord of hosts: I will save my people from the east country and from the west country; and I will bring them to live in Jerusalem. They shall be my people and I will be their God, in faithfulness and in righteousness . . . For there shall be a

sowing of peace; the vine shall yield its fruit, the ground shall give
its produce, and the skies shall give their dew; and I will cause the
remnant of this people to possess all these things . . . These are the
things that you shall do: Speak truth to one another, render in your
gates judgments that are true and make for peace, do not devise
evil in your hearts against one another, and love no false oath; for
all these are things that I hate, says the Lord . . . Many peoples and
strong nations shall come to seek the Lord of hosts in Jerusalem,
and to entreat the favor of the Lord.

Otherworldly visions entered into the tradition along with the apocalyptic genre, found in prototypical forms in Isaiah, Zechariah, Ezekiel, and Joel, and in its fullest sense in Daniel and several apocryphal texts. In an apocalyptic text, a story is told in which an otherworldly being mediates a revelation to a human seer, disclosing future events involving transcendent reality that is directly related to human temporal existence.[1] Most of these texts were likely written during social crises for communities that were oppressed or marginalized, and the visions often included the judgment and toppling of the powers under whom they were suffering.

The book of Daniel, set during the Babylonian exile, was likely written during a period of persecution under Antiochus IV Epiphanes (175–163 BCE). Daniel is visited by angelic mediators and given visions of a future of geopolitical powers in turmoil, all of them ultimately failing. These visions functioned to help the book's audience see their marginalization and suffering through eschatological faith and hope: they could be assured that just as the kings of Babylon faded away, so too would contemporary oppressors, because God ultimately controls human history and God's people will be vindicated: "But the holy ones of the Most High shall receive the kingdom and possess the kingdom for ever—for ever and ever" (Dan 7:18).

The kingdom of God is a central theme in biblical eschatology. It entered the Hebrew canon fairly late, especially in Daniel, but became central to much of the New Testament, particularly the eschatology of the Gospels. In all the synoptics, Jesus's ministry opens with an announcement of the kingdom (Matt 4:17; Mark 1:14–15; Luke 4:21). Each of the Gospels has a particular emphasis in relation to the kingdom: its urgent imminence in Mark, its less urgent but no less awaited *parousia* in Luke, the judgment that it will bring in Matthew, and that which is already realized in John.

---

1. This description is a paraphrase of several criteria agreed upon in the late-1970s by a working group of the Society of Biblical Literature and has since been published many places, especially in the writings of John J. Collins and Adella Yarbro Collins.

Many Christians who have heard these texts, and indeed prayed daily for the kingdom to come, have been inured to its blatantly political meaning. We should not forget that, even from its earliest beginnings in Scripture, the kingdom of God "is the most political of Christianity's doctrines."[2] In Jesus's proclamations of the kingdom, the political visions of the prophets and seers of Israel are constantly implied, if not directly quoted.

In the Gospels, eschatological teachings about the already-not-yet kingdom are interspersed with hints of apocalypticism, especially in Mark's famous "little apocalypse" in chapter 13. And the New Testament famously ends with the unmistakably apocalyptic and undeniably political text of Revelation. Like generations of Jews before them, early Christians under Roman occupation and persecution found in apocalyptic their ability to relativize an oppressive empire's pretensions of ultimate power in the light of God's sovereign reign over the cosmos. Some New Testament scholars have also found apocalyptic theology not only in the texts most clearly identified with the apocalyptic genre, but also in perhaps the least suspected place: the letters of Paul. It has recently been argued that modern, European understandings of politics and justice so colored Christian interpretation of Paul as to create a contractual, instead of more appropriately "apocalyptic," framework for his theology.[3]

Eschatology in Augustine and Aquinas

Many have identified Augustine and Aquinas as two of the most influential political theologians in the Christian tradition. Alongside Scripture, their writings have been the most consistently drawn upon (and critiqued) in the political theologies of the Christian West. And we find in their writings, as well, the absolute centrality of eschatology to political theology.

Augustine's *De Civitate Dei* is widely considered to be the seminal postcanonical text in Christian political theology. Its retelling of human history as a tale of two cities, one limited to and by its orientation toward this-worldly reality, and the other eternal in its desires and *telos*, is a thoroughly eschatological tale of the already and the not yet. God's sovereignty is already visible within human history, and the meaning of history has been made manifest in the Christ event; those whose lives are shaped by love for God live here and now in ways that participate in what is ultimate

2. Scott, "Kingdom Come," 159.
3. Campbell, *Deliverance of God.*

and eternal. Yet God's sovereignty is not yet visible in many earthly realities; those whose lives are shaped by love for self can only participate in fatally partial versions of all that is true and good. To the Roman pagans who are blaming Christians for the unraveling of the empire, Augustine's apologetic message is that in the Christ event, history's meaning is already revealed, and anything good about the empire was a faint shadow of the true justice and peace that is eternal. To the anxious Christians who had equated God's sovereignty in history with the empire and its embrace of Christianity, Augustine's pastoral message is that the empire is not the kingdom of God but merely one manifestation of the earthly city.

William Cavanaugh has argued persuasively that political theologies falter when they ignore the eschatological complexification of space and time found in Augustine's two cities. Modern political theologies have tended to map the roles of church, state, and civil society so that "the element of time has been flattened out into space,"[4] whereas Augustine "did not map the two cities out in space, but rather projected them across time."[5] We speak of "spatial carving up of society into spheres of influence" in ways that divide what is public and political from what is sacred and religious. By contrast, Augustine emphasized that "there is no division between earthly goods and heavenly goods, secular and sacred."[6] Both cities make use of the same goods, but for different purposes, with different orientations.

> The reason that Augustine is compelled to speak of two cities is not because there are some human pursuits that are properly terrestrial and others that pertain to God, but simply because God saves in time. Salvation has a history, whose climax is in the advent of Jesus Christ, but whose definitive closure remains in the future. Christ has triumphed over the principalities and powers, but there remains resistance to Christ's saving action. The two cities are not the sacred and the profane spheres of life. The two cities are the *already* and the *not yet* of the kingdom of God.[7]

Thomas Aquinas, likewise, cannot be understood in relation to politics apart from an understanding of the pervasive role of eschatology in his thought. "Aquinas teaches that eschatology is not a highly speculative appendix to any systematic theology, but a dimension characteristic of and inherent in

4. Cavanaugh, "From One City to Two," 57.

5. Cavanaugh, "From One City to Two," 59.

6. Cavanaugh, "From One City to Two," 57.

7. Cavanaugh, "From One City to Two," 70.

all God-talk."[8] Although Aquinas was never able to complete his work on eschatology in the *Summa Theologiae*, eschatology nevertheless pervades the *Summa* as well as his "political" writings elsewhere (if indeed there is any coherence at all in parsing apart "the political" from anything else in premodern theology—or any theology, for that matter). The eschatological vision of beatitude—the taking up of all creation into perfect union with and glorification by God—is what rightly gives order to all of human life in history, including human government. The way governments can now be oriented toward this ultimate reality is through providing the conditions for the establishment of the common good. Equally, the way governments descend into perversions of their intended purposes is through the pursuit of some *telos* other than the common good. Tyranny arises when a government's *telos* is the private good of those wielding power instead of the common good of all those on behalf of whom they rule.[9]

Matthew Lamb has argued that it is precisely in the common orientation of their eschatologies that we may best learn to see past the calcified stereotypes of Augustine as the pessimistic Platonist and Aquinas as the optimistic Aristotelian.[10] Lamb's contention is that both Augustine and Aquinas have a "sapential eschatology," that is, eschatology that "depends upon a faith-illumined knowledge and wisdom about the *telos* or end of the whole of redeemed creation."[11] Aquinas follows Augustine, who already "understood that the eternal divine presence creates and sustains the totality of time in all its concrete particularity and universality. Eternity does not denigrate time, but creates it." According to Augustine, especially in the *Confessions*, God is

> the fullness of Being as Presence freely creating, sustaining, and redeeming the universe and all of human history in the Triune Presence. All extensions and durations, all past, present, and future events, are present in the immutable and eternal understanding, knowing, and loving who are Father, Word, and Spirit. The eternal God creates the universe in the totality of its spatio-temporal reality. There is no before or after in God's eternal presence.[12]

8. Leget, "Eschatology," 381.

9. Aquinas, *De regimine principum*, 1.II.

10. Lamb, "Wisdom Eschatology in Augustine and Aquinas," 259.

11. Lamb, "Wisdom Eschatology in Augustine and Aquinas," 259.

12. Lamb, "Wisdom Eschatology in Augustine and Aquinas," 264.

In both Augustine and Aquinas, "sapential eschatology overcomes tendencies toward instrumentalizing both nature and divine revelation," as it recognizes that "the revelation of eschatology in Holy Scripture supernaturally fulfills the finality of the created universe rather than simply destroying and negating it in a final conflagration, as if that were all."[13] In this way, Aquinas in particular builds upon patristic interpretations of eschatological and apocalyptic texts in Scripture "as revealing the transformation of the whole of creation so that it fully manifests the divine wisdom, beauty, and goodness. This contrasts with those who view these passages as involving or portending widespread devastation or ultimate doom."[14]

This sapiential approach to eschatology, which holds together the doctrines of creation and eschatology through the category of *telos*, has already often been noted for its centrality to the political theology of Aquinas, because his work on both natural law and the common good are so dependent upon it. As Gregory and Clair have noted, similarities in Augustine often go unnoticed in political theology because of our preoccupation with a single book in *De Civitate Dei*.[15] Matthew Lamb's attention to the *Confessions* draws us beyond this preoccupation and demonstrates the same matrix of creation, eschatology, and teleology at work in Augustine.

Eschatology and the Emergence of Political Theology

Having noted the centrality of eschatology in the politics (and indeed politics in the eschatology) of Scripture, as well as two of the most authoritative theologians of Christianity in the premodern West, we are not then surprised to find that in modernity, when appeals to the authorities of tradition went decisively, if only partially, out of fashion, Christian eschatology became decidedly less political.

One key aspect of the emergence of political theology as a distinct discipline in the mid-twentieth century was a desire to bring eschatology and politics back into conversation within academic theology. Catholic theologians had long been in the habit of treating eschatology as an appendix to dogmatics, and even there it generally only dealt with what would happen at the end of time and in the life to come. "Eschatology" was a collection of brief descriptions of the second coming, the resurrection of the dead,

13. Lamb, "Wisdom Eschatology in Augustine and Aquinas," 265.

14. Lamb, "Wisdom Eschatology in Augustine and Aquinas," 274.

15. Gregory and Clair, "Augustinianisms and Thomisms."

final judgment, heaven, and hell. Protestant theologians, meanwhile, had been rejecting the importance of such external matters in favor of existential meaning. Eventually the task became the stripping of ancient trappings from the essence of Christianity, and eschatology was an obvious target for the demythologizers.

By the early to mid-twentieth century, the doctrine of eschatology began to resurface. Protestant theologians like Schweitzer and Barth, and Catholics like Rahner and Balthasar, brought eschatology to the center of their work. European political theology seized upon this renewal and insisted both that Christian politics must be eschatological and that eschatology must be political. Jürgen Moltmann boldly proclaimed that while the theologians had been tinkering with death-of-God theology and demythologizing, the Marxists had cornered the market (if you will permit me the ironic wordplay) on hope. In *Theology of Hope* (1964), Moltmann sought to answer the valid critiques of Marxism while rejecting its a-theological materialism. The biblical narrative of redemption, from the exodus through the resurrection of Jesus and pointing toward the coming kingdom, is the narrative of this hope—a hope for this world, within history.

Eschatology was also at the heart of Metz's new political theology. In *Theology of the World* (1968), he argued that Christian hope in the promises of God is neither a passive waiting on a future, otherworldly reality which is ready-made for us, nor is it the encounter with a purely existential present reality. Instead, Christian eschatology is "productive and militant" in relation to the "emerging and arising" future. "The eschatological City of God is now coming into existence, for our hopeful approach builds this city."[16] However, this is not a mere "militant optimism. Nor does it canonize man's own progress."[17] The eschatologically motivated church is not a separate society, but "the liberating and critical force of this one society."[18]

Theologies of liberation also emphasized eschatology, many of them drawing on the work of Moltmann in particular, reinterpreting his message in the European context for application in their own contexts. An entire chapter of Gustavo Gutiérrez's groundbreaking work in Latin American liberation theology, *A Theology of Liberation* (1971), was dedicated to "Eschatology and Politics." Here, Gutiérrez argued,

16. Metz, *Theology of the World*, 94.
17. Metz, *Theology of the World*, 97.
18. Metz, *Theology of the World*, 96.

The life and preaching of Jesus postulate the unceasing search for a new kind of humanity in a qualitatively different society. Although the Kingdom must not be confused with the establishment of a just society, this does not mean that it is indifferent to this society. Nor does it mean that this just society constitutes a "necessary condition" for the arrival of the Kingdom, nor that they are closely linked, nor that they converge. More profoundly, the announcement of the Kingdom is realized in a society of fellowship and justice; and, in turn, this realization opens up the promise and hope of complete communion of all persons with God. The political is grafted into the eternal.[19]

James Cone, in *Black Theology and Black Power* (1969), rejected the otherworldliness of eschatologies that encourage the oppressed to embrace their current sufferings in light of future rewards. Instead, he argued, eschatology must relate future hope to present realities. "Black Theology insists that genuine biblical faith relates eschatology to history, that is, to what God has done, is doing, and will do for his people."[20]

Realized eschatology became a focus of feminist political theology in this generation. A conviction that traditional eschatology was premised upon a strict dualism of body and soul, earth and heaven, which valued only the latter, led many feminists to reject any notions of eternity and afterlife, interpreting the kingdom of God as an entirely this-worldly reality. In *The Radical Kingdom* (1970), Rosemary Radford Reuther argued both that social radicalism in the West has historically been motivated by Christian eschatology and that the gospel of the kingdom of God for today is a message of radical sociopolitical transformation.

In response to the interiorizing and demythologizing of eschatology in Europe, and to the spiritualizing otherworldliness of eschatologies in contexts of oppression in the Americas, the first generation of political theologians sought to reclaim both the centrality of eschatology in theopolitics as well as the centrality of theopolitics in Christian eschatology.

19. Gutiérrez, *Theology of Liberation*, 134–35.
20. Cone, *Black Theology and Black Power*, 126.

The Millennium and the Kingdom

The Millennium in Modern North Atlantic Christianity

Intriguingly, while eschatology was on hiatus in most of academic theology—Ernst Troelsch famously commented that in nineteenth-century theology, the office of eschatology was usually closed—North Atlantic Protestantism of popular practice was awash in millenarian eschatologies.

One way to describe variations in Christian eschatologies is by their interpretation and employment of the idea of the millennium: an eschatology is millenarian or amillennial depending on whether or not it focuses on the thousand years of peace on earth described in Revelation 20. Millenarian eschatologies can be either postmillennial (viewing the millennium as an age that human agency can usher in, which will end with the second coming of Jesus) or premillennial (viewing the millennium as an age that Jesus ushers in through his return to earth, and during which he reigns over earth). In very broad terms, postmillennialsm has been associated with political optimism and activism for social transformation, while premillennialism has been associated with political pessimism and a fatalist view of the increasing social evils of the world during the present age.

To many British Christians in the nineteenth century, the extraordinary social upheaval surrounding the French Revolution, accompanied by the precipitous decline of the Catholic Church in France, seemed to chime with the events in the apocalyptic texts of Daniel 7 and Revelation 13. Many became convinced that the end was near, and new forms of premillennialism arose. By the 1830s, there were numerous British conferences, periodicals, and societies focused on biblical prophecy. A movement of Anglican clerics in the beginning, by the second half of the century, premillennialism was more concentrated in Baptist churches and in new dissenting groups such as the Irvingites and Plymouth Brethren.

The nineteenth century was also a time of millenarian ferment in America in ways that were perhaps more fragmented and diverse, including forms of postmillennialism, some from the continuing influence of Jonathan Edwards and others from the new Disciples of Christ movement, and forms of Adventism in Millerite, Mormon, and Shaker groups, as well as the Oneida Community. "America in the early nineteenth century was drunk on the millennium. Whether in support of optimism or pessimism, radicalism or conservatism, Americans seemed unable to avoid—seemed bound to utilize—the vocabulary of Christian eschatology."[21] John Nelson Darby and other British premillennialists began to tour North America in the 1860s, and the following decades saw an explosion of premillennialist conferences and the founding of premillennialist Bible institutes for the training of evangelical clergy.

British premillennialists and their American followers had a pessimistic view of the world, a deep conviction that everything—including the church—was getting worse. For them, God's dealings with humanity over the course of history could be described as a series of dispensations; in each dispensation, God had used new means by which to reach humanity and to test their obedience. But every time, humans failed the test and were judged by God. In the current dispensation, the test is whether Jesus Christ will be accepted as savior.

The literalist approach of dispensationalists to the Bible in general, and prophecy in particular, led to constructions of elaborate end-time chronologies. As the end of the present age winds down, immorality, apostasy, poverty, natural disaster, and war will all increase. Suddenly, at an unpredictable moment, the true church will be raptured. The Beast will rule over the revived Roman Empire and the Antichrist will be head of the apostate church. Jews, having returned to the land of Israel "in unbelief," will rebuild the temple, only to have it desecrated by the Beast when he turns on Jews and the church, demanding to be worshiped. There will be a Great Tribulation, characterized by unprecedented human suffering. A remnant of 144,000 Jews will accept Jesus as Messiah and evangelize the suffering world. Two-thirds of them will be martyred. The apostate church will be destroyed. Finally, the empire of the Beast will attack Israel in the battle of Armageddon, but Jesus Christ will return as military victor to destroy the Beast's forces, judge the Gentile nations for their treatment of Israel, be accepted as Messiah by all surviving Jews and Gentiles, gather the remaining Jews of the world into the land of Israel, and establish the kingdom, ruling the world from Jerusalem for one thousand years.

Some approaches to dispensationalism focus only on its pessimism about the current age and neglect the key fact that dispensationalist visions of the millennium are utopian. During the millennial age, there will be absolute fairness, equality, and justice in all social and political structures and practices. Human bodies will thrive in an existence without illness or violence. The earth and all its inhabitants will thrive as the soil becomes

---

21. Sandeen, *Roots of Fundamentalism*, 42.

more productive and animals no longer kill one another. Every aspect of embodied, social reality will be transformed.

The Kingdom of God in Dispensationalist Fundamentalism, Postmillennial Liberalism, and Reinhold Niebuhr

Soon after the turn of the twentieth century, Protestant eschatologies fell in line with emerging fault lines between liberalism and fundamentalism in America. Diverse forms of nineteenth-century evangelicalism, when faced with the perceived enemies of modernism and liberalism, coalesced into a more uniform fundamentalism, and dispensational premillennialism became the eschatology of choice for fundamentalists.

Historians of American Christianity have long debated the impact of dispensationalism on the theopolitics of fundamentalism and evangelicalism. Some have posited that dispensationalist eschatology single-handedly transformed the socially progressive and active evangelicals of the nineteenth century into the inwardly focused and socially conservative fundamentalists of the twentieth century.[22] Others have argued that the transformation was neither that stark nor attributable to eschatology alone.[23] While the latter, more nuanced argument has become something of a consensus, it is nonetheless agreed that the social fatalism inherent in dispensationalism contributed to the social inertia evident in some aspects of fundamentalism and evangelicalism in America.

Pessimism about the inevitable worsening of social evil, natural disaster, and theological error as the current age continues is an obvious contributor to inertia, and the one most widely discussed, but it is not the only relevant aspect of premillennialism. In its dispensational form, premillennialism teaches that the current age is actually a pause in divine time, a temporal parenthesis when God's plans are on hold. This is because Jesus Christ came to earth to announce and establish the kingdom of God, but Jesus was rejected and the kingdom was postponed. We thus live in a mysterious age, not foretold by the prophets, during which the church exists. The prophetic time line will resume at the end of this age, when the true church is raptured and all end-time prophecies are fulfilled in the

---

22. Timothy Smith called this "the great reversal," and his thesis was carried forward by Martin Marty and Timothy Weber. See Smith, *Revivalism and Social Reform*; Marty, *Righteous Empire*; and Weber, *Living in the Shadow of the Second Coming*.

23. See especially Marsden, *Fundamentalism and American Culture*.

tribulation, second coming, and millennium. Israel collectively rejected Jesus and put the kingdom on hold, so we await every aspect of the social, embodied transformation of the kingdom until the millennium arrives, the kingdom is established, and all Israel is saved. In the meantime, the work of the church is to convince Gentiles to accept Jesus as savior, thus the current era is marked by individual, spiritual salvation instead of social transformation.

On the other side of the divide, postmillennialism was the eschatology of liberal Protestantism. Perhaps the most influential factor in the solidification of its prominence was the social gospel movement. Though most were not concerned with a literal thousand-year period, liberal Protestant postmillennialists viewed the coming century as the time in which God's intentions for society might be fully realized, especially through the reform of industrial labor. This postmillennial drive for social transformation, and its optimism in the ability of American Christians to establish the kingdom of God on earth, would lead to the naming of what is still the leading popular magazine for liberal Protestants: *The Christian Century*.

In the theology of the social gospel, primarily shaped and articulated by Walter Rauschenbusch, the kingdom of God as sociopolitical reality intended for the here and now was the central theme. Rauschenbusch said of the kingdom of God, "This doctrine is itself the social gospel."[24] He defined the kingdom as "the Christian transfiguration of the social order," specifying that the "Church is one social institution alongside of the family, the industrial organization of the society, and the State. The Kingdom of God is in all these, and realizes itself through them all."[25] The kingdom of God, on this view, was the progressive improvement of society, and the establishment of this progression was the purpose of the church. "The institutions of the church, its activities, its worship, and it theology must in the long run be tested by its effectiveness in creating the Kingdom of God."[26]

Reinhold Niebuhr, a frequent contributor to *The Christian Century*, was famously and deeply critical of all forms of turn-of-the-century optimism, and particularly the social gospel. His criticisms, however, were not eschatological. For Niebuhr, the error of the social gospel was its attempt to apply the ethic of Jesus to the social realm. "The ethic of Jesus was," he said, "a personal ethic," an ideal that is "too rigorous and perfect to lend

24. Rauschenbusch, *Theology for the Social Gospel*, 131.
25. Rauschenbusch, *Theology for the Social Gospel*, 145.
26. Rauschenbusch, *Theology for the Social Gospel*, 143.

itself to application in the economic and political problems of our day."[27] One of the main functions of this division between the personal and political in Niebuhr was his contention that the *agape* ethic of Jesus could only function interpersonally and is dangerous if applied sociopolitically, where coercive justice must be the norm. This marginalization of the politics of Jesus has rightly been the focus of many critiques of Niebuhr's work. In my view, it renders much of his work unusable in contemporary political theology.[28]

Perhaps surprisingly, then, we find something rather more usable and fruitful in a slightly lesser-discussed corner of his work where he does explicitly treat eschatology and the kingdom of God, in *Faith and History* (1949). In the chapter "The End of History," Niebuhr targeted the rather nonspecific (and not entirely accurately rendered) categories of "Platonism" and "utopianism." The former he identified with an annulment of history by the eternal, and the latter with an optimism in progressive improvement within history that denies the transcendence of the eternal.[29] Laying aside the possibilities for debating his interpretations of Platonism and utopianism, we find something interesting in his assertion that a key feature of Christian eschatology is that "[b]y the symbol of the resurrection the Christian faith hopes for an eternity which transfigures, but does not annul the temporal process."[30]

How much more interesting this insight might have been if applied to the most popular eschatologies of his day, dispensational premillennialism on the one hand, and liberal postmillennialism on the other. In dispensationalism, we see that the eternal purposes of God can only be accomplished within history when Christ comes to violently claim control over earth against and in spite of all human action to the contrary; it is utter divine annulment of human history preceding the millennium. In postmillennialism, we see an unchecked optimism in the ability of human action to fulfill God's eternal purposes in the present age, so that human politics rather than eternity transfigures our temporal existence.

Niebuhr also rightly relates the church to the sociopolitical content of the kingdom when he says, "it is that community where the Kingdom of God impinges most unmistakably upon history because it is the community

27. Niebuhr, "Ethic of Jesus and the Social Problem," 30.
28. See Phillips, *Political Theology*, ch. 4.
29. Niebuhr, *Faith and History*, 269–70.
30. Niebuhr, *Faith and History*, 269.

where the judgment and the mercy of God are known, piercing through all the pride and pretensions of men and transforming their lives."[31] This is neither the church of dispensationalism, a parenthetical holding station awaiting the true meaning of history that has not yet arrived, nor is it the church of the social gospel, one institution alongside all the others that have analogous roles in fulfilling the meaning of history here and now.

According to Niebuhr, this church "must be sacramental." The sacraments "symbolize the having and not having the final virtue and truth," and through them the church can "express its participation in the *agape* of Christ and yet not pretend that it has achieved that love."[32] Precisely where Niebuhr was so wrong about Jesus of Nazareth, in relation to the content and function of *agape*, he is piercingly right about the presence of Christ in the sacraments. By that presence we are infused with love and hope, and by that presence we are made keenly aware of God as the source of true love and hope; these are divine realities in which we participate, not abilities that we can claim to have mastered. In the Eucharist, we find that "[w]hat lies between the memory and the hope is a life of grace, in which the love of Christ is both an achieved reality in the community, and a virtue which can only be claimed vicariously," and thus "the supreme sacrament of the Christian church . . . is filled with this eschatological tension."[33]

In Search of a Normative Apocalypse

Narrating Apocalyptic Politics

Many theologians would argue that the reason Niebuhr's eschatology is so helpful here is precisely because it is eschatology and not apocalyptic; all normative uses of apocalyptic engage in the annulment of history that he described.[34] I believe such theological dismissals of apocalyptic trade in a misguided narration of what "apocalyptic" is and how it functions politically.

In his famous and standard treatment of the "revolutionary millenarians and mystical anarchists of the middle ages," historian Norman Cohn (1957) described the apocalypses as texts that foretell "immense cosmic

31. Niebuhr, *Faith and History*, 271.
32. Niebuhr, *Faith and History*, 273.
33. Niebuhr, *Faith and History*, 273.
34. See, e.g., Mathewes, *Theology of Public Life*.

catastrophe" and that functioned in their original contexts as "nationalist propaganda."[35] On this reading, apocalyptic feeds a paradigm in which an existing demonic power must be overthrown by God's saints, who will then be in charge of the culmination of history.[36] Thus "apocalyptic" movements are those with a dualistic view of contemporary sociopolitical realities and which identify themselves with the good people of God who are being called, with great urgency, to overthrow the evil powers at work in relation to some impending catastrophe and the end of history.

Note how little these descriptions of apocalyptic resonate with the descriptions of biblical apocalyptic with which this chapter began. What drives our identification of social and political movements as "apocalyptic"? Rather than identifying movements that resonate with apocalyptic texts and their original functions, we identify movements that we feel comfortable judging as fanatical in terms of their self-identification in relation to good and evil and that in some way involve a conviction about the nearness of the end of time—even though neither moral dualism nor the end of time are identifying characteristics of the apocalyptic genre. In other words, perhaps it is much more the case that we define apocalyptic as a dualistic approach to sociopolitical realities in light of a belief in history's immanent end, because this is the theopolitics we have seen in so many disturbing sociopolitical movements. Perhaps we even then read this definition back into the original texts, making our conclusions inevitable: apocalyptic in all its forms is dangerous and should be shunned in normative political theology.

As one would expect, historical, anthropological, and sociological work on apocalyptic has moved on since Cohn. In his now standard historical text, Paul Boyer (1992) identified the widespread preoccupation with aspects of eschatology in modern America, which often appealed primarily to apocalyptic texts, not in terms of "apocalyptic" but "prophecy belief."[37] Boyer's more careful and informed overview of the apocalyptic genre and the apocalyptic texts of the Bible made it clear that what has so often been driving the imagination of the end in modern America is not that people's orientation to events has been "apocalyptic," in that it mirrors the orientation and function of the apocalypses of Scripture. Instead, it has been the

---

35. Cohn, *Pursuit of the Millennium*, 20.

36. Cohn, *Pursuit of the Millennium*, 21.

37. Boyer, *When Time Shall Be No More*.

interpretation of these texts as literal prophecies of coming events and the
reading of contemporary life in relation to this "prophecy belief."

It has also been widely recognized that when "apocalyptic" is used in
the popular sense, as it was in Cohn, there is nothing peculiarly Jewish or
Christian about it, and nothing that necessarily ties it to ancient apocalyptic texts. While there are clearly still groups of this sort who do appeal to
the apocalyptic texts of Scripture in both Judaism and Christianity, there
are also these sorts of "apocalyptic" movements in many places in modernity and contemporary politics, in Islam, in new religious movements in
both East and West, in supposedly "secular" discourses, and in Catholic
movements that primarily appeal to contemporary Mariology rather than
ancient apocalyptic. It is also recognized that some of these movements
are obviously politically dangerous (the Branch Davidians, Aum Shinrikyo)
while others carry on in relative ease within society (sects within Baha'i and
Adventism).[38]

My argument here is neither that apocalyptic texts do not contain
some jolting, destructive, and violent imagery—some clearly do—nor that
Jews and Christians have not or do not today perpetrate politically abhor-
rent things that they directly relate to the apocalyptic texts of Scripture—
they clearly have and do. Nor is it that the ways in which "apocalypticism"
goes wrong should not be a concern of normative political theologies—
they should. Rather, the point is that the use of the label apocalyptic in ways
that bear no direct relationship to the overarching contents and functions
of apocalyptic texts, nor necessitate any connection whatsoever with them,
puts us in danger of falling into syllogistic ways of approaching apocalyptic
in political theology: apocalyptic is the orientation of x, y, and z groups
historically; x, y, and z groups were politically dangerous; apocalyptic in all
its forms is politically dangerous.

Eschatology, Apocalyptic, and Creation

How then can we constructively articulate the normative employment of
apocalyptic in political theology? Thus far, we have considered the roles of
eschatology and apocalyptic in Scripture, Augustine, Aquinas, first-gener-
ation political theologians, nineteenth- and twentieth-century North Atlantic Protestantism, and narratives of "apocalyptic" movements. I suggest

38. See Robbins and Palmer, *Millennium, Messiahs, and Mayhem.* See also Hunt,
Christian Millenarianism from the Early Church to Waco.

that at least four variables have been at work throughout these political eschatologies that have determined whether or not apocalyptic was being employed in constructive and faithful ways that should be embraced as normative.

1. *Defining "Apocalypse."* The first factor in whether apocalyptic is inherently divergent from normative political theology or central to it is one's definition of apocalypse.[39] Both popular movements that dangerously wield apocalyptic and scholars of theology and religion who value eschatology over against apocalyptic because the latter is necessarily dangerous assume the popular meaning of apocalypse, which is the cataclysmic end of the earth and human history. Those who are able to imagine constructive theopolitical employments of the apocalyptic emphasize the original meanings of apocalypse: unveiling, revelation, disclosure. To embrace apocalyptic as a genre as well as a theological mode of reasoning about and relating to our common lives in this world is not, then, to long for an otherworldly future that eclipses and annuls this world and its history, which is the reasonable anxiety of those who oppose the apocalyptic in politics. Rather, it is to embrace an openness to seeing what is ultimate in the world and the social order through dramatically calling status quo power claims into question.

In her recent book about early Jewish apocalyptic, Anathea Portier-Young has described the function of early apocalypses in precisely these terms. She argues that the early Jewish apocalyptic visionaries did not engage in "a flight from reality into fantasy, leading to radical detachment from the world or a disavowal of the visible, embodied realm." Instead, they were resisting imperial domination and manipulation, "challenging not only the physical means of coercion, but also empire's claims about knowledge and the world." Through their apocalypses, "[T]hey did not flee painful and even devastating realities, but engaged them head on."[40] This engagement was both a matter of resisting imperial accounts of reality (epistemic manipulations) and resisting imperial ordering of life (bodily dominations). The apocalypses both "answered terror with radical visions of hope" and issued in programs of "radical, embodied resistance rooted in covenant theology and shaped by models from Israel's Scriptures as well as new revelatory paradigms."[41]

---

39. I introduced this first variable elsewhere. See *Political Theology*, ch. 8.

40. Portier-Young, *Apocalypse against Empire*, xxii.

41. Portier-Young, *Apocalypse against Empire*, xxiii.

2. *Apocalyptic Analogies*. This leads us directly into a second variable: whether or not the uses of apocalyptic are analogous to the functions of those texts in their original contexts. Definitions of apocalypse as cataclysm have also often been wedded with an understanding of apocalyptic as literal readings of events in apocalyptic texts applied with urgency to current events. These employments of apocalyptic are dangerous because literal readings are in place at two levels: the texts are read as literal predictions of events, and contemporary politics are read as literal fulfillments of those predictions.

When the original function of apocalyptic texts is understood in terms of directly engaging oppressive powers by disclosing realities that transcend them and give oppressed communities hope, the task shifts from watching current events for signs of literal fulfillment of predictions to watching the world for analogous sites of oppression where analogous visions of resistance and hope should be employed.

The political theologians of the first generation of the discipline embodied many of the best aspects of apocalyptic in the ways in which they questioned status quo power arrangements in the Christianity of their contexts, and in the ways in which they often gave resistant voices to oppressed and marginalized communities. In the historical examples we have considered here, they are by far the best examples of apocalyptic analogy; which is ironic considering how many of them rejected the "apocalyptic" in favor of the "eschatological" along with most theologians of their day.

3. *Eschatological Apocalyptic (and Apocalyptic Eschatology)*. However, these political theologies often fared less well in relation to a third variable, the relationship between apocalyptic and wider eschatology. In their rightful protests against both internalizing existentialist readings and spiritualizing futurist readings of eschatology, and against the devaluing of this world and the bodies in it, the political and liberative theologies of mid-century tended to opt for overrealized eschatologies. Normatively employed apocalyptic must be situated within the wider category of Christian eschatology and governed by its tension between the already and the not yet. Failure to understand apocalyptic in this context creates failure to be faithful in our political engagements, whether this failure is one of inertia because the apocalyptic vision is of the unrealizable not yet or one of zealotry because the apocalyptic vision is of the urgent already.

On the one hand, dispensationalist convictions about sociality, embodiment, and politics inevitably worsening until their redemption, which will only be possible in the divinely controlled millennium, have led generations of Christians to believe that in this age the gospel's transforming power comes only in human hearts through individual conversion and salvation, and this must be the sole mission of the church; sociopolitical transformation exists only in the not yet. On the other hand, one of the most determinative dynamics at work in many "apocalyptic" groups whose politics most of us can agree are genuinely dangerous is the utter erasure of the not yet, so that certain aspects of the visions of some biblical apocalyptic (or indeed, regime-changing and earth-ending visions from any number of sources) are associated with a literalist and uncritical immediacy to current contexts. Because of this urgency, and the loss of all patience and prudence that is demanded of us by the not-yet, "apocalyptic" reasoning involves jettisoning what is "normally" morally normative; because an unparalleled event is about to occur, normal moral reasoning must be abandoned.

But even if we grant that apocalyptic needs the already-not-yet tension of eschatology, can we argue that eschatology needs apocalyptic? Why hold on to these ancient and sometimes troubling texts and try to find normativity in them? I believe the contents of the canon give us our cue here. There is a reason why we have the peaceful visions of the messianic age in Isaiah along with the radical toppling of kingdoms in Daniel. There is a reason why in one Gospel the kingdom seems urgently imminent, in another Gospel it seems near but not so urgently near, and in another Gospel it seems already to be here. There is a reason why there are measured, pastoral texts on eschatology as well as the Apocalypse of John. The presence of all these types of texts and modes of eschatology in the canon alert us to the very many ways imbalance between or within them have caused problems in history, as well as how their interrelation can be fruitful, particularly politically.

4. *The Doctrine of Creation.* Eschatology in general, and apocalyptic in particular, must also be grounded in the doctrine of creation, by which I mean, along with Augustine and Aquinas, an understanding of creation not as the point of the world's origin, but as the reality within which our world and its history exist. The abundant, loving, life-giving goodness of God creates and sustains all that is, continuously. This understanding of creation makes the link between creation and eschatology clear: God's own life is the ever-present source and goal of our lives. We live from, in, and toward God.

It is important to ground eschatology in this understanding of creation for at least two reasons. First, the eschatologically visionary community must be drawn ever back to its conviction that the earth and all that constitutes our embodiment are good creations issuing from the Goodness of the Creator God. This grounding of eschatology prevents the apocalyptic strand from the tendencies that it can otherwise have that annul the world and devalue the body. Second, the meaning of political existence must be found in both the doctrines of creation and eschatology, held in relation to one another. Holding together the questions of how and why we are created as political animals and how our creation is intertwined with the creation of earth and all its other creatures, with questions of how our politics will be consummated in the eschaton and how all creation will be transformed and glorified, allows a coherent theopolitics to be formed in relation to both the source and the goal of politics, which are both in God.

Last Things and Things That Last, or Ends and the End

James William McClendon Jr. taught that eschatology was not simply the ✗
doctrine of last things, but the doctrine of things that last. Christian political theology has always been ordered by visions of the last things, and in its best employments theopolitical eschatology has focused on things that will last. Eschatologies that align themselves with the traditional sources of Aquinas, and more recently highlighted aspects of Augustine, focus on these things that last: the wisdom, beauty, and goodness in and for which human sociality and all creation came into being and toward which it moves in anticipation of the eternal beatific vision in which all creation will be taken up into the infinite wisdom, beauty, and goodness of God. Eschatologies that emerged in the twentieth century after the era of the doctrine's neglect focus on these things that last: the equality, community, and freedom in and for which human sociality was created and toward which earthly powers must be pointed in light of the ultimate justice of the kingdom of God.

And yet, practitioners in these two streams tend to be radically dismissive of one another. My argument in favor of the normative employment of apocalyptic in theopolitics is perhaps, in the final analysis, an argument in favor of attending to both streams with utter seriousness, without denying the weaknesses in both or the ways in which they cannot be reconciled to one another.

Augustine recognized that there are not so much "spiritual" things that will outlast "worldly" things, rather the things that will last, which are taken up into eternity, are all things oriented toward God and ordered by desire for and love of God. What happens in the end, according to both Augustine and Aquinas, is not the end of all that has gone before, but the judgment of the ends of all that has gone before.

CHAPTER 2

Political Theology and Theological Ethics (2021)

This chapter was originally published in a section with the title "Christian Ethics and Political Issues." Like most syllabi and textbooks in Christian ethics, the volume in which it was published was divided into methodological sections and "issues" sections, with "political" as one type of issue alongside medical/bioethical, sexual, economic, justice, and environmental issues. Nothing is wrong with this way of organizing subjects in Christian ethics, *per se*, and I have often written and taught within similar frameworks. Done well, it can be clarifying. However, it can also be argued that situating the political as a type of "issue" in ethics is not without its problems—problems that bring into relief some of the differences between the frameworks of Christian ethics and Christian political theology.

Framing of the political as an ethical issue bears the distinct marks of (1) modern academic divisions of disciplines based on the sciences, where theology is the "pure" work of "theory" and politics is one among several areas where "social ethicists" do the work of "application," and (2) modern decisionistic and quandary-based approaches to ethics in which the horizon for consideration of politics is a set of problems that need solutions. I will take each of these in turn.

Politics as Application

The volumes of Thomas Aquinas' *Summa Theologiae* are neatly divided into three parts. For contemporary learners and practitioners of Christian ethics or systematic theology, the order of these three sections may seem strange. First comes his treatment of theology proper: the Trinity and the doctrine of creation. Second comes his moral theology. And third is Christology, the church, and the sacraments. Why are the doctrinal or dogmatic topics straddling the moral or ethical topics in this way? This was an intentional assertion by Aquinas that moral theology is not separate from doctrine. As D. Stephen Long has noted, "His discussion of Christian morality in the second part of his *Summa Theologiae* both depends upon the first part, where he sets forth the doctrines of the Trinity and creation, and requires the third part on Christology, church and sacraments for its completion."[1] Many scholars of Aquinas have commented upon the irony and inaccuracy of the practice of studying the second part in isolation from the others, as if he wrote the second part for the ethicists and the other two parts for the theologians. Aquinas, obviously, knew no such distinction, and he intentionally positioned his work against the medieval precursors of such distinctions.

Interestingly, even if we do pursue the inevitably detrimental and anachronistic attempts to divide his work into dogmatic and moral theology, if we then further attempt to isolate his political work, we find it stretches across the parts of the *Summa*.[2] The political is not a topic or issue isolated to the second part. As with the classical philosophers and the early theologians before him, in the work of Aquinas any consideration of what is good and ultimate will necessarily be infused with considerations of the political. An attempt to isolate the political thought of most patristic authors would be equally detrimental and anachronistic. The political is a thread woven throughout the letters, apologies, sermons, and treatises of early Christianity.

Sharp distinctions between ethics and systematic theology arose in the modern era, and most prominently in Protestant theology. Even the idea of "moral theology" would become associated with Catholicism as opposed to the "Christian ethics" of Protestantism. Protestant ethics would eventually be further divided into theological ethics and social ethics, in which the

---

1. Long, "Moral Theology," 457.
2. See, e.g., the excerpts in Dyson, *Aquinas: Political Writings*.

Bible and Christian tradition remained valid sources for the former, but the social sciences became the guide for the latter. By the end of the twentieth century, Protestants (particularly in America) who were studying or teaching Christian approaches to the political were most likely doing so under the heading of "social ethics" and with methods informed substantively by social science. Joining with social science in applying frameworks (and philosophical assumptions) from modern scientific method, Christian ethics too was divided into its pure or fundamental pursuits (theological ethics) and its applied pursuits (social ethics). The social ethicist's work was to identify social problems, understand them through social-scientific methods, and offer remedies to them through the application of Christian principals and norms derived from pure theology. Critics of this pure/applied division note how not only subject matter, but also source material was wrenched apart in such disciplinary separation; so-called theological ethics has often neglected experience as a source, and so-called social ethics has often neglected both Scripture and tradition.

Protestants were not entirely alone in drawing such distinctions. From the Council of Trent until the present, there has been an official distinction in Catholicism between dogmatic or fundamental theology and moral theology. However, these were framed in relation to Aristotelian distinctions between intellectual and moral virtues instead of pure and applied scientific methods. The sources of reason, Scripture, and tradition were equally important for both discourses, and experience would come to be recognized as a source in more recent versions of both. From the late-nineteenth century there also developed a distinct tradition of Catholic social teaching (encyclicals as well as other official teaching and conciliar documents and statements), Catholic social thought (wider treatment of the issues of social teaching by theologians and lay people), and Catholic social tradition (diverse forms of activism, organizing, and policy-making related to social teaching). Whereas politics became the purview of the social ethicist in Protestantism, Catholic learners and teachers of Christian approaches to the political might do so under any one of this wide variety of headings, or a combination thereof.

One consequence of these disciplinary and methodological divisions, most prominently in Protestant social ethics, but doubtless too in some forms of moral theology and Catholic social thought/tradition, was that the political largely ceased to be a category for constructive, systematic, or doctrinal work—the kind of work done in pure or fundamental disciplines.

Practitioners became far less concerned—if at all—with theologies of the political or politics of the theological and focused instead on political "issues" in ethics and the moral life. Questions of the meaning and nature of human sovereignty and its relation to the sovereignty of God, and questions of the place of the political in creation, for examples, became eclipsed by the pursuit of identifying and addressing social problems.

POLITICS AS PROBLEM

Christian ethicists very rightly should, of course, seek to identify and address social problems. This is not in question. However, a good deal of the game of moral theology has already been given away if the political is always already perceived in terms of problems to be solved. Conceptualizing the political as an issue to be addressed by practitioners of methods of application not only divides social ethics from theology, splitting the four sources of Christian ethics between its pure and applied forms instead of holding them in conversation with one another, but also sets the parameters of the discourse as one of social problems which need moral solutions. These social problems may be correctly identified and meaningfully addressed, and they may be exactly the sorts of problems to which Christian ethicists' attention should be turned; my argument here is not to question the *validity* of the social-problem-solving discourse, but to question its *sufficiency*. Focusing *solely* on the status quo of readily identifiable problems and seeking to come to decisions about their status and/or remedies can prevent the Christian ethicist from understanding the subject theologically, removing from access crucial theological resourcing for the entirely valid task of addressing problems.

Both the identification of politics as a problematic issue and the agenda of making decisions about the quandaries it poses constrain moral imagination as well as praxis. One aspect of retrievals of the virtue tradition in recent Christian ethics has been an awareness of the limitations of quandary-based frameworks, which have largely been determined by approaches which assume that there is a clear set of quandaries facing the ethicist, and the task is employing either deontological or consequentialist methods for making these difficult decisions. Advocates of virtue ethics not only critique deontology and consequentialism on their own terms, but also note how the employment of the two methods in late modern Christian ethics results in ethical enquiry being overdetermined by the difficult/

exceptional instead of the everyday, the quest for the best method of reasoning instead of the best way of life, the focus on doing instead of being, and the removal of teleology and other wider questions of meaning and ultimacy from moral reasoning. The possible subjects of enquiry into the political as well as methods, sources, and horizons for political enquiry are limited in all these ways when the political is reduced to quandaries.

The same can be said of any number of topics that are likewise treated as "issues" (read: problems to be addressed by "applied ethics"). Two examples will illustrate the insufficiency of the issues-and-problems framework. Consider the framing of medical ethics. There is a conventional set of issues which Christian ethicists consider: reproduction, contraception, and abortion; euthanasia, assisted suicide, and end-of-life; medical resources and access; and new medical technologies. The vast majority of the conversation is framed as: here is a professional medical practice; should Christians be for it or against it? And what method will you employ in order to decide? Theological questions about the meaning of health and suffering, life and death, interdependence and the common good, sexuality and procreation are marginalized. Not only should such questions be pursued in their own right, apart from the ethical, but attention to them is also crucial for good moral reasoning in medical ethics.

Consider, as another example, the female body in Christian ethics. In light of feminist and womanist insight, it becomes clear that the female body only ever enters into most Christian ethics in relation to problems to be solved; women's bodies become "issues" in sexuality, reproduction, contraception, and biotechnology. Both the agency of women and the wonder and dignity of the female body are eclipsed. Our moral horizon, limited by the social-problem-solving discourse has only furthered the objectification of women, making our bodies sites of debate instead of agency and sites of concern instead of awe.

Situating politics as a set of issues—problems to be addressed through applied or social ethics—is equally detrimental to our theological understandings and praxis of the political as it has been in these two examples. One of the ways in which this has come to light in recent decades, and I argue one important way to recover some of what has been lost in our disciplinary silos and decisionistic methods, is through the work of political theology.

THE RISE OF POLITICAL THEOLOGY

Critiques of social ethics as an applied social science and of ethics as quandary-based decisionism are by no means new. Both critiques have been central to the work of prominent theologians on both sides of the Atlantic since at least the 1980s. Importantly, during these decades social science theory and practice have also taken post-structuralist turns, giving rise to internal critiques of the positivism in which these disciplines arose and first influenced Christian ethics. Perhaps it should come as no surprise, then, that interest in political theology as a discipline has become so prominent in the wake of the ascendency of critiques of the positivism and structuralism of early social science, and of the limitations of ethics-as-quandary. More scholars and students are crossing previously strict disciplinary boundaries and coming to political theology from both theology and ethics (not to mention philosophy of religion and religious studies, or the many versions of political theology outside the theological disciplines).

Political theology, broadly defined, has always been part of Christian theology. Using this sense of the phrase, Cavanaugh and Scott offer a good guiding definition:

> Theology is broadly understood as discourse about God, and human persons as they relate to God. The political is broadly understood as the use of structural power to organize a society or community of people . . . Political theology is, then, the analysis and criticism of political arrangements . . . from the perspective of differing interpretations of God's way with the world.[3]

Throughout Scripture and the traditions of Christian theology, political theology has been a consistently central task. It emerged as a distinct discourse in the twentieth century, by the name "political theology" in Germany as theologians grappled with Christian complicity in the Third Reich and its Holocaust, but also in Latin America as theologian-priests faced down the church's complicity in poverty and political oppression, and in North America as Black and woman theologians began to bring their voices to the fore. Emerging as distinct movements in the mid-twentieth century, these discourses eventually converged and inspired later discourses (such as public theology, various liberative and contextual theologies, and various postliberal theologies) which came to be studied and practiced under the umbrella title, "political theology." Around the turn of the twenty-first

---

3. Scott and Cavanaugh, *Blackwell Companion to Political Theology*, 2.

century, new courses, textbooks, academic journals, and professional groups began to appear, more firmly establishing political theology as a distinct academic discipline.

But is political theology the answer? Can political theology open up the restricted horizons of politics as an issue in Christian ethics? Or, perhaps the first question is whether the diagnosis offered here should be answered by pointing to better ways of doing ethics. Do we need political theology or do we just need better moral theology? My answer is yes. We need, and many Christian ethicists and moral theologians currently do, better ethics than I have described above. And I join with many proponents of virtue ethics who would argue that the critical and constructive retrieval of virtue employed through the use of all four sources of Christian ethics goes a long way toward overcoming the limitations of approaching politics as a set of problematic issues. However, I also argue that political theology is something distinct from politics in Christian ethics and that both political theology and Christian ethics are needed disciplines and tasks.

Ted Smith has argued that ethics is limited to a horizon of "moral obligations that play out within immanent networks of cause and effect."[4] He argues that although the "immanent frame" of ethics may be able to "accommodate many kinds of moral reasoning"—including deontology, consequentialism, and virtue—it cannot readily imagine, recognize, or accommodate that which exceeds the frame and/or is exceptional to it.[5] Ethicists are often caught within this immanent frame, arguing about whether or not this or that action or practice can be justified within it—seeming to be on opposite sides of something, but actually arguing two sides of the same frame.

Political theology is not a remedy in that somehow we will agree more about politics if we do political theology instead of ethics. Rather, political theology can, and indeed must, exceed the ethical frame and can therefore reveal what is being missed within it, what it cannot account for, and what questions are worthy of enquiry beyond moral justification. However, although political theology may exceed the ethical, it cannot erase the ethical. Remember, as we have already established in this chapter, early and medieval Christian theology did not divide the two tasks or understand them to have differing practitioners. Contemporary constructs of academic discipline and specialization may separate Christian ethics and political

4. Smith, *Weird John Brown*.
5. Smith, *Weird John Brown*, 5.

theology, and we must understand them as distinct tasks, but we must not conceive of them as tasks to be chosen between. Both ethical work in politics by moral theologians and the work of political theology are needed. Consider, as an example, the specific case of violence: how it can be, is, and should be treated in Christian ethics and political theology.

Violence in Christian Ethics and Political Theology

The vast preponderance of Christian ethicists' thinking, writing, and teaching on the subject of violence focuses on a single question (and subsidiary questions thereof): whether or not Christians can justifiably employ violent means. Thus courses and textbooks in Christian ethics focus primarily on debates concerning just war and pacifism and perhaps (in the American context, especially) capital punishment. There is a quandary to be solved: Christians have a duty to apply both the norms of love and justice, but we do not agree on whether the application of these norms rules out the use of violence, or sometimes tragically requires violence as a last resort, or positively commands violence for preservation of the social order. The ethicist and the student of ethics are meant to choose a side, to determine their own solutions to the violence quandary.

Much influential work has already been done on how the debate between just war and pacifism has obscured the common theological ground of peace and taken focus away from practices of peacemaking.[6] This is one—and a particularly crucial—way of opening up the moral imagination beyond the binary options of just war and pacifism, and to my mind it is one of the most important topics in teaching Christian ethics. This is one example of how better practice of ethics goes a long way toward answering the limitations I have described. However, the introduction of peacemaking theories does not necessarily move us beyond the ethical quandary; it *may* only add another option for addressing it.

By contrast, entirely different questions are on the table in political theology. For example, why is it that virtually all Christian theology has assumed that the state can and indeed must employ violent means? Whether this assumption is framed as a prelapsarian intention for human government or a postlapsarian requirement of sin, and whether it is argued that Christians can or cannot themselves be the executioners of state violence, state violence *per se* was virtually unquestioned in Christian tradition until

6. Especially Stassen, *Just Peacemaking*, and Wink, *Engaging the Powers*.

the late-twentieth century. Political theologians question state violence and ask why Christian tradition (including its traditional pacifist strands) has not questioned this deep-seated assumption.

For some political theologians, this work begins with the politics of doctrines of creation, eschatology, and anthropology. Is violent conflict part of our natural state, due to original sin? Is violence a consequence of the fall which is overcome in Christ, and if so, what does that mean this side of the eschaton? Some political theory, both explicitly theological and not, situates itself in a trajectory of thought from Augustine through Luther then Hobbes and Machiavelli. This trajectory sees the basic condition of the world and humanity as violence that government must control in order to minimize. John Milbank famously argued in *Theology and Social Theory* for an "ontology of peace" in Augustine, which insists that the world and humanity were created in, and move toward a future of, peace. In Milbank's argument, this is a theopolitical conclusion, not an ethical conclusion; it is an argument about the character of human sociality, not about just war versus pacifism.

A different theopolitical enquiry can be seen in the work of William Cavanaugh, whose political theology has been particularly influential in opening up questions about state violence apart from questions of just war versus pacifism. In *Theopolitical Imagination*, Cavanaugh argued against the idea that the modern secular state rescued Western civilization from the inherent violence of religion, questioning both the historical accuracy of this narrative as well as identifying its alternative soteriology—a false theology in which the state is seen as the savior of the people. In *The Myth of Religious Violence*, Cavanaugh extended this argument significantly, identifying and arguing against the myth that religion is a transhistorical and transcultural feature of human life, essentially distinct from "secular" features such as politics and economics, which is peculiarly dangerous and inclined to violence and therefore must be controlled by restricting religious access to public power.

The myth, Cavanaugh argues, depends on three assertions (or assumptions): (1) that there is something called "religion" that has existed across time in all human cultures and is separable from other facets of human life such as politics; (2) that "religion" is peculiarly prone to violence and/or that the preponderance of human violence has its genesis in "religious" impulses; and (3) that the modern secular state is the antidote to "religious violence" (asserted either in terms of the rise of the secular nation-state saving the West from the chaos of religious wars, or in more recent terms of the spread of Western liberal secularism as able to save the West from the religious violence of Islam).

The problem with this narrative is not that it ascribes violent behavior to "religious" people, groups, and movements—Cavanaugh does not by any means deny that Christians, among others, do indeed act violently. According to Cavanaugh, however, "The problem with the myth of religious violence is not that it condemns certain kinds of violence, but that it diverts moral scrutiny from other kinds of violence. Violence labeled religious is always reprehensible; violence labeled secular is often necessary and sometimes praiseworthy."[7]

The issues at stake are, resolutely, always and already both theological and political. The myth enshrines a counter-soteriology, giving the secular state savior status; and the myth authorizes violence instead of reducing it.

> In foreign policy, the myth of religious violence serves to cast non-secular social orders, especially Muslim societies, in the role of villain. They have not yet learned to remove the dangerous influence of religion from political life. Their violence is therefore irrational and fanatical. Our violence, being secular, is rational, peace making, and sometimes regrettably necessary to contain their violence. We find ourselves obliged to bomb them into liberal democracy.[8]

M. Shawn Copeland's work in political theology demonstrates how questions and discourses outside the ethical frame help us look beyond the state in our political considerations of violence. As Maureen O'Connell has noted, "Copeland clearly stands in the tradition of post-Holocaust German political theology," so that for her, "[f]aith is not merely a private experience, but a profoundly political one animated by the dangerous memory of Christ." Yet she "'troubles' the Euro-centric waters of political theology from her location at the crossroads of sexism and racism," realities that have "marked her own body in a way that the Holocaust never marked the German Christian bodies of Metz or Moltmann or Soelle."[9]

In *Enfleshing Freedom*, Copeland considers the "wounding, then, terrorizing of the Black body through commodification, abuse, and lynching," relating these experiences to the "dangerous memory" of the crucifixion and our formation in the Eucharist to see clearly and to transform the

---

7. Cavanaugh, *Myth of Religious Violence*, 121.

8. Cavanaugh, *Myth of Religious Violence*, 4.

9. O'Connell, "Disturbing the Aesthetics of Race," 234.

violence of the world.[10] Copeland names the violence of the slave trade's removal of Black subjectivity through the erasure of social and familial bonds, objectification of persons-as-commodities, high expectations of both performance and morality (without the resources of decent nutrition and living conditions, much less the dignities of education or freedom), as well as the obvious physical violence of the transport, selling, raping, and beating on which the trade depended. She goes on to describe, in devastating historical narratives, the continued terrorizing of Black bodies after slavery in the era of lynching. The demand of this history of violence, Copeland insists, is solidarity—not a vague, liberal feeling of empathy, but a specifically eucharistic solidarity.

> Our daily living out, and out of, the dangerous memory of the torture and abuse, death and resurrection of Jesus Christ constitutes us as his own body raised up and made visible in the world. . . . Eucharist is a countersign to the devaluation and violence directed toward the exploited, despised black body . . . In spatial inclusion, authentic recognition, and humble embrace of different bodies, Eucharistic celebration forms our social imagination, transvalues our values, and transforms the meaning of our being human, of embodying Christ.[11]

Key to Copeland's argument is that the Eucharist is not thereby reduced to the ethical. She reminds us that "the crucial social consequences of Eucharist can never overtake the real presence the Eucharist effects." The heart of eucharistic solidarity and resistance to racist violence is not located in human action, but in divine action. "In our presence, the Son of Man gathers up the remnants of our memories, the broken fragments of our histories, and judges, blesses, and transforms them. His Eucharistic banquet re-orders us, re-members us, restores us, and makes us one."[12] Eucharist is *the* performative liturgy; the slave traders and the lynch mobs performed idolatrous anti-liturgies.

Lest the ethicists begin to worry that such political-theologizing detracts from or discourages concrete political praxis, we only need to consider Copeland's enactment of solidarity in relation to the Black Lives Matter movement. In a call to action to her fellow political theologians, urging us to take concrete actions in relation to racism, she wrote,

10. Copeland, *Enfleshing Freedom*, 110.
11. Copeland, *Enfleshing Freedom*, 127.
12. Copeland, *Enfleshing Freedom*, 128.

We do political theology because we want to collaborate in a most fundamental way in healing and creating relations in history and society. We want to coax forward a different sociality. Our contribution is to think and rethink, in light of the divine promise of an eschatological future, the manner and effects of the fragile yet resilient webs of relations that constitute the reality in which we live. Our work is to open that sociality to the desire, hope, and loving expectation of something (even Someone) transcendent.[13]

Perhaps we would not articulate our reasons for doing Christian ethics much differently. My argument is not that as Christian ethicists and political theologians we are doing unrelated tasks for opposing reasons, rather that we can perform these two discourses within related yet differing frameworks, drawing on related but differing sources, aiming toward related yet differing horizons. Christian theology continues to need the immanently normative frames of the ethicists as well as to be opened to that which exceeds them in the practices of theopolitics.

13. Copeland, "Memory, #BlackLivesMatter, and Theologians," 2.

CHAPTER 3

Future Hope/Present Realities:
A Sermon on the Life and Work of James Cone (2016)

> You shall not wrong or oppress a resident alien, for you were aliens
> in the land of Egypt. You shall not abuse any widow or orphan. If
> you do abuse them, when they cry out to me, I will surely heed
> their cry; my wrath will burn, and I will kill you with the sword,
> and your wives shall become widows and your children orphans.
> If you lend money to my people, to the poor among you, you shall
> not deal with them as a creditor; you shall not exact interest from
> them. If you take your neighbor's cloak in pawn, you shall restore
> it before the sun goes down; for it may be your neighbor's only
> clothing to use as cover; in what else shall that person sleep? And
> if your neighbor cries out to me, I will listen, for I am compassion-
> ate. (Exod 22:21–27 NRSV)

I wonder if you have any particularly clear memories of waiting for a par-
ent who was late coming home from work? For most of us, these will have
only been moments of annoyance at late dinners or moments of hurt feelings due to promises not kept. In his most recent book, *The Cross and the
Lynching Tree*, James Cone shares his memories of waiting for his father on
days he came home late from work. For Cone, these are memories of deep
fear—sitting by the window, longing to see the headlights of his daddy's
pickup truck, hoping that he was alive and not hanging dead from a tree
somewhere in the darkness. James Cone grew up in the American state of

Arkansas, where he was born in 1938. His childhood was infused with the bitter and all-encompassing realities of racial inequality and oppression, including the terror of routine beatings, rapes, and murders perpetrated by white people against African Americans without fear of prosecution. On those days when he waited by the window, his mother would assure him that God would take care of his father, but young James had his doubts. Where was God in all the suffering and death he had already witnessed, even as a young child?

Cone went on to beat the odds stacked against him and made his way to university, where he would choose to write his first essay on the question "Why do people suffer?" He went on to postgraduate study of theology, earning his doctorate and becoming a lecturer. Lingering questions about suffering remained, and he found that the more deeply he believed in God, the more difficult it became to sustain his faith.

These internal, personal questions were given new purchase when they were met with the questions of his students. As he narrated in his book, *God of the Oppressed*, Cone entered classrooms as a young lecturer armed with extensive knowledge of the great thinkers of the Christian West, and he found their theology falling flat before his Black students both in relation to the depths of their experiences of suffering and in relation to the depths of their personal experiences of Jesus Christ. He began to realize that it would not do to understand and expound upon theology as a set of abstractions.

James Cone was at the leading edge of a new moment in Christian theology—a moment in which he and soon other Black theologians, Catholic theologians in Latin America, and post-Holocaust theologians in Germany—were taking a long, hard, painful look at suffering in their contexts—the suffering of Black people, of those in poverty, and of Jews—and asking where, in God's name, had Christianity been amidst all this suffering. And what they all converged upon in this "moment," stretching from the late-1960s to the early 1980s, was the forgotten centrality of liberation in Christianity—they insisted that God identifies with and acts in liberating solidarity amongst those who are oppressed, and that Christianity was tragically failing through its complicity in oppression. Liberation theology, in all its many forms, was born.

James Cone was the founding theologian of Black liberation. In 1968, three years after earning his PhD and two months after the assassination of Martin Luther King Jr., he began to write the first book of the movement,

Black Theology and Black Power. Of his many subsequent books, the best known are *A Black Theology of Liberation* (1970), and *God of the Oppressed* (1975). He remains an active lecturer and writer and is distinguished professor of systematic theology at Union Theological Seminary in New York. He has recently said of his work, "If I have anything to say . . . it is rooted in the tragic and hopeful reality in which I was born and raised. Its paradoxes and incongruities have shaped everything I have said and done."[1]

In Cone's first book, *Black Theology and Black Power*, we see a Black theologian of the 1960s caught in the paradox and incongruity of the social movements around him. Cone was deeply drawn to the hopeful, nonviolent resistance movement led by Martin Luther King. He was also deeply drawn to the revolutionary Black Power movement led by Malcolm X. He argued that, although King's movement was explicitly Christian and the Black Power movement often explicitly rejected Christianity as the white man's religion, the Black Power movement was, in fact, "Christ's central message to twentieth-century America"[2] because, "In Christ, God enters human affairs and takes sides with the oppressed. Their suffering becomes his; their despair, divine despair. Through Christ the poor man is offered freedom now to rebel against that which makes him other than human."[3]

In *God of the Oppressed*, Cone went on to make his case for this liberationist view of God, arguing that the God of the Bible is God of the oppressed, who sides with and liberates those at the margins of existence. God takes the side of the enslaved Hebrews and delivers them from Egypt, then instructs them (as in this evening's reading from the book of Exodus) to likewise be people who side with the oppressed and not become oppressors themselves—the reading closes with the promise that if they become oppressors, God will hear the cries—God will choose the side of—the oppressed.

Cone's argument here was not one merely about the content of Scripture, but also about the interpretation of Scripture and the sources of theology. Scripture could never be the source of theology alone; the revelation of God as God of the oppressed was also a revelation of the experience of the oppressed as a source for theology. A Black theology of liberation must begin with the experience of Black persons in the world. Part of the failure of academic theology up to that point had been the failure to recognize that

1. Cone, *Cross and the Lynching Tree*, xv.
2. Cone, *Black Theology and Black Power*, 1.
3. Cone, *Black Theology and Black Power*, 36.

such theology was unwittingly drawn from the source of the experiences of, and thus served the purposes of, whiteness. Christian theology had ceased to be Christian theology and had become instead White theology. Naming and exposing White theology would be one of the central tasks of Black theology.

Some of Cone's most provocative and compelling critiques of White theology came in his second book, *A Black Theology of Liberation*, in which he roundly mocked the false, imagined Jesus of comfortable white suburbia, and stated—with a naked refusal of ambiguity—"What need have we for a white Jesus when we are not white but black? If Jesus Christ is white and not black, he is an oppressor, and we must kill him."[4]

The extraordinary longevity of James Cone's academic career, which has already spanned over fifty years and is not yet at its end, has meant that he has continued to work alongside at least two subsequent generations of Black theologians, many of whom are indebted to his work but have made distinctly critical decisions to take different directions in their own work. In the generation after Cone's early work, one of his shortcomings which was most clearly recognized was his unacknowledged sexism. Cone's early Black theology, claiming Black experience as its source, arose very distinctly from the experience of a Black man. Black men and white women were able to make inroads into academic theology before Black women, and when Black women arrived in the academy, many resoundingly declared that neither Black theology nor white feminism spoke for them—the experiences and voices of Black women were nowhere to be found in either discourse. A more recent criticism of Cone's work from the latest generation of Black theologians is that it has suffered from working within the confines of the imaginary constructs of race—that instead of questioning the historical production of the constructs of "white" and "black," he assumed them and allowed them to be determinative.

Many other important critical questions have been asked and will continue to be asked about the liberationist theologies which arose in the 1960s, with Cone's Black liberation theology at the forefront. Such questions should be pursued, but never as mechanisms by which we can imagine we have escaped from James Cone's piercing analysis and pressing demands. His work requires us to take seriously the reality that theology arises in contexts from experience—no theology comes from nowhere. And his work requires us to take seriously that not only in the American South of

4. Cone, *Black Theology of Liberation*, 117.

his youth, but in the majority of the historical and the present realities of Christianity in the West, theology has been constructed in alignment with power and privilege instead of in solidarity with the poorest and most oppressed—those with whom God identified himself in Jesus Christ, and for the good of whom God has always called people to live in the world.

"The real scandal of the gospel is this," writes Cone, "humanity's salvation is revealed in the cross of the condemned criminal Jesus, and humanity's salvation is available only through our solidarity with the crucified people in our midst."[5]

Amen.

---

5. Cone, *Cross and the Lynching Tree*, 160.

CHAPTER 4

A Surprising and Mysterious Unity:
A Pentecost Sermon (2021)

When I agreed to preach on this date long ago during lockdown, I had no idea I would have the privilege of preaching our first in-person sermon since September. It is indeed a privilege, and I am so cheered to see you all here together, though there are some who are still dispersed and joining us online, to whom we send all our love.

How amazing that we come back together for the first time as we celebrate the day on which the Spirit of God came among the gathered community of the first followers of Jesus and empowered them to continue his ministry on earth. That day on which, having seen the risen Lord ascend into heaven, the disciples are watching and waiting, gathering and readying themselves for what comes next. And the Holy Spirit comes, and they are alight as with fire, and when they speak, everyone gathered in Jerusalem from all over the known world can understand them in their own languages.

The story of Pentecost in Acts 2 is often read alongside the story of the Tower of Babel in Genesis 11,[1] in which the people, all speaking one language, try to build a tower to the heavens until God causes them to speak in many tongues and they cannot understand one another. Pentecost is often

---

1. Although I do not follow him at every point, much of the framing of this sermon arose from a reading of Brueggemann's treatment of the Babel narrative in his Genesis commentary.

read as the redemption of Babel; the man-made tower of pride ascending into heaven which was punished by the confusion of languages is overcome because Jesus himself has ascended into heaven and the Spirit has reunited all the languages.

There is something to these readings, but there are also many questions to ask. Centuries of men with various levels of power have interpreted the sin of Babel as pride, and this goes along with a common school of thought which says that pride is at the heart of all human sin. But with the benefit of a few generations in which we have been able more easily to hear the theological voices of women and of people who are not in power, we must question whether the heart of human sinfulness is, in fact, pride. When people who have been marginalized and oppressed assert pride in who God has created them to be, this is anything but sinful; and telling women, people of color, and queer people to resist pride is simply telling them to stay in their place.

So perhaps instead of reading Babel as a story about the sin of pride which is punished with disunity and Pentecost as a story about the restoration of unity—perhaps another reading would be of two stories of two different kinds of unity: the predictable unity imposed by human will and the surprising unity gifted by the Holy Spirit.

On this reading, we see in Babel an idolatry of unity imposed by human will. The tower is a symbol of reifying and worshipping the kind of unity that humans in power persistently enforce. It is the kind of unity which says that what makes us strong is being alike, and that being alike means being like those who are in power. This is unity-as-homogeneity, defined and enforced by those in power, at the expense of those who must conform. It is the completely predictable unity of empire and patriarchy and racism—and of all those who solidify their own power by ascribing non-being to those without power.

On this reading, we see at Pentecost the refreshment that blows like wind where unity is the gift of the Holy Spirit. This is a unity of diversity; the unity of the body with all its different parts; the unity of diverse gifts given by the Spirit for our mutual flourishing.

The Spirit does not come on Pentecost and replace the many diverse languages with a single language; it does not simply reverse the creation of many languages at Babel. Instead, the Spirit comes and brings unity of hearing one another within the diversity of languages.

On this reading, we have to wonder whether we have misread the confusion of languages at Babel as punishment. Was God punishing people for their pride by taking away their ability to work together to build the tower? Or was God perhaps jolting them out of an oppressive version of unity so that they might become open to truer, God-breathed unity?

In our Gospel reading from John (15:26–27, 16:4b–15), Jesus says that the Spirit will guide the disciples into all truth, because the Spirit will speak only what the Spirit hears, and the Spirit will glorify Jesus by giving to us from all that which belongs to the Father, which also belongs to Jesus. Jesus says the Spirit will "take what is mine and declare it to you."

This is one of the most explicitly Trinitarian texts in all of Scripture. The Triune God is an absolute unity of being in three persons, and it is in the unity of the Trinity that we see the sort of unity for which we are created and intended—the surprising, mysterious unity which is the gift of the Holy Spirit.

The unity given by the Holy Spirit is *surprising and mysterious*, which means that we cannot hear this story as simply reinforcing familiar truisms of easy, lazy liberalism so that we who consider ourselves all in favor of diversity and inclusion can simply pat ourselves on the back anew. The Spirit of God has always been at work in the world calling out, gathering, and including the least expected, the least attractive, the least recognized, *the least*. And however enlightened and inclusive and liberal and progressive any of us may understand ourselves to be, there are still those people who are, in our books, *the least*. There are still those whom we consider somehow beyond the pale, and there are still those whom we consider not at all, because they remain invisible to us. But if we listen for the rustling of the Spirit of God in this world, if we look for the Spirit's enlivening flames, we will find ourselves called into surprising, mysterious unity with those very people.

Notice that in the Gospel reading, Jesus says that the Spirit will "speak" and "declare," which means that our most important role in relation to the Spirit is to listen. In fact, in the Pentecost story, the emphasis is not only on how the disciples spoke in different languages, but on how those listening were able to *hear*: "each one *heard* them speaking in the native language of each. Amazed and astonished, they asked, '. . . how is it that we *hear*, each of us, in our own native language?'" And as the story goes on, Peter preaches his famous sermon and those who *hear* are "cut to the heart."

Can we hear God's Spirit today? Are we listening? Will we allow the wind of the Spirit to guide us where we do not expect to be led and the flame of the Spirit to shine light on the people we do not want to see? Will we allow God to jolt us out of all our attempts to enforce false unities, and gift us with true unity—unity which does not overcome our difference, but teaches us how to hear God and one another in the midst of our diversity?

In the name of the Father, the Son, and the Holy Spirit. Amen.

II. Ethnography of Eschatology: American Christian Zionism

CHAPTER 5

Charting the "Ethnographic Turn" (2012)

It is a sunny, spring Sunday morning in the heartland of America. People are streaming into an enormous church building. They are serenaded by praise music played through speakers that line the walkways from the multiple parking lots. At the building's main entrance, they pass a large fountain, above which is suspended a huge golden globe. Friendly church members meet them at every door with a handshake or a hug. As they enter the sanctuary, they pass a large wall made of white stone imported from the Holy Land. Tall, black, metal letters are mounted on the wall reading, "Pray for the Peace of Jerusalem." The sanctuary's 2,600 seats are steadily filling as a band, choir, and praise team lead worship. Everyone on stage is dressed in Israeli blue and white. Large video screens project words to the songs over a background image of the Western Wall of the Temple Mount. Everyone is singing in Hebrew, hands lifted high. "Meshiach! Meshiach! Meshiach!"

Today is this congregation's annual Israel Awareness Day. It is the culmination of a month of sermons and classes on topics related to biblical prophecy and current events in the Middle East. It is a day when the church's four worship services focus especially on the modern nation-state of Israel as the center of God's intentions for human history. The entire local community—particularly its Jewish members—are invited to come in the evening for an extravaganza of pro-Israel music, dance, drama, and prestigious speakers. Last year it was Israeli paratrooper Shaol Amir and

Texan pastor John Hagee. Tonight it will be a local rabbi and former Israeli ambassador Dore Gold.

This morning's sermon is on Ezekiel's vision of the dry bones. Pastor George has some props on stage to drive the point home. The dry bones, he explains—standing next to and gesturing toward a pile of bones—is Israel scattered, the Diaspora. When the bones began to rattle, that was the rise of the Zionist movement. Pastor George unveils a classroom skeleton and says that the bones began to come back together when Jews immigrated to the Holy Land in the 1940s. The skeleton received its muscles and flesh—it became a body—when Israel became a state. Then Pastor George tells the congregation what comes next. He says,

> Now . . . here's what's happening. Let me give you this picture so you can understand why we . . . stand with and support Israel as a nation and encourage our government to do the same, because . . . God says, "I'm going to set watchmen [on the wall]. I'm gonna put people in position so that they would pray that the next step will happen to the nation of Israel." What's the next step? The breath of God. God's spirit breaths on them and they come alive to accept their Messiah.

This was one Sunday morning in the Christian Zionist congregation which I recently studied. As a Christian ethicist who has engaged in an "ethnographic"[1] study of a Christian congregation, I hope to make two contributions to the conversation represented by this volume. First, growing out of my own process of searching for reasons and ways to do this research, I hope to chart the wider conversations of which this one is a part; namely, the turn of theologians toward "ethnography" as well as concurrent and convergent shifts in anthropology and sociology. Second, I hope to relate this conversation to the discipline of theological ethics, illustrated by the ethnographic research I conducted in order to write a piece of theological ethics on the topic of American Christian Zionism, and to demonstrate why theologians (and theological ethicists, in particular) should be studying Christian congregations.

A certain type of Christian Zionism is a formative influence—in widely varying degrees—for virtually all American Protestants who are anywhere right of center theologically. Many have concluded that the

---

1. I am not entirely comfortable with theologians using the word "ethnography," but I will return to this below. For now I will allow it to stand as it does in the literature being discussed.

influence of Christian Zionism contributes significantly to Americans' misunderstandings of the Middle East and their support for foreign policies which have tragic consequences in that region. Moved by these realities and by desire for a just peace in the Middle East, I decided several years ago to study American Christian Zionism, but I was not sure how or where to begin. It was suggested to me that I read Randall Balmer's book, *Mine Eyes Have Seen the Glory: A Journey into the Evangelical Subculture in America.* Balmer's book narrates his visits to several evangelical and fundamentalist congregations, communities, and institutions across the United States. I found the book compelling, and the idea of spending time in a Christian Zionist congregation seemed to be the ideal way forward. However, it was immediately apparent to me that it would be a serious task to determine what it would mean for a theological ethicist to do this type of research.

This led me to an exploration of the ethnographic turn many theologians have been proposing, as well as to shifts in the social sciences that could make theological use of social-scientific methods somewhat less problematic and potentially more interesting across the divisions between the disciplines. I developed the following account of various sources and streams of the ethnographic conversation among theologians and how these relate to the social-scientific disciplines as well as to existing theological disciplines of congregational studies.

In 1974, the American Baptist theologian, James McClendon, published *Biography as Theology*, in which he argued that utilitarianism (and other forms of quandary-based or what he called "decisionistic" ethics), as well as Christian realism, had run their course and proved insufficient. He insisted that Christian practitioners of ethics should have intentionally theological methods, and he suggested that the task of theology is "investigation of the convictions of a convictional community," in which those convictions are discovered, interpreted, criticized, and if needed and possible, transformed. One task of theological ethics thus conceived should be reflection upon exemplary lives that embody the convictions of a community, which he called "biography as theology." As an illustration of this proposal, McClendon reflected upon instantiations of the doctrine of atonement in the lives of four individuals.[2] He was not suggesting that atonement (or any other doctrine) is only "a motif embodied in contemporary life stories,"

---

2. Dag Hammarskjöld, Martin Luther King Jr., Clarence Jordan, and Charles Ives. In the 1994 edition, McClendon's new preface described how feminism had since transformed his theology and how regrettable he found it that he only included lives of men.

rather that while doctrines can be stated propositionally, such statements must be tested through "contact with lived experience."[3]

One of McClendon's former students, Theophus Smith, sought to widen the task from individual biography to ethnography of communities, and his work in African American Christianity has focused on the community as "socio-political performer of strategically selected biblical stories and images."[4] Smith was influenced in this work not only by McClendon, but also by other theologians who have been central to the ethnographic turn in America, including Roman Catholic scholar of missions and theology and culture, Robert Schreiter.[5] Chief among these, of course, is George Lindbeck and his argument in *The Nature of Doctrine* for a "cultural-linguistic model" of theology. Lindbeck described the existing models of theology as (1) cognitive-propositional, which views religion as a cognitive enterprise and doctrines as propositional descriptions of objective truth; (2) experiential-expressive, which views religion as personal experience and doctrines as expressions of inward feelings, attitudes, or orientations; and (3) the combination of these two attempted especially by ecumenical Roman Catholics. Lindbeck offered his cultural-linguistic model as an alternative that, learning from contemporary anthropological, sociological, and philosophical literature, views religion as resembling cultures with languages and forms of life in which doctrines function as rules of discourse, attitude, and action.

McClendon was also influential for Stanley Hauerwas, who has advocated the narrative description of specific congregations as an important task for both theologians and congregations themselves. He has suggested that sociological and anthropological methods may be used fruitfully as long as congregations' stories are learned and told with normative, not merely descriptive, intentions. Hauerwas has emphasized that social-scientific methods are unhelpful to theologians only when they are employed so uncritically or rigorously as to "methodologically preclude the theological claims necessary for the church's intelligibility."[6]

Among British theologians, the work that parallels the widespread influence on this conversation which Lindbeck's *The Nature of Doctrine* had previously, is of course Milbank's *Theology and Social Theory*. Milbank

3. McClendon, *Biography as Theology*, 149.

4. Smith, "Ethnography-as-Theology." See also, *Conjuring Culture*.

5. Author of *Constructing Local Theologies*.

6. Hauerwas, "Ministry of a Congregation," 130.

argued that various forms of secular thought are actually pagan or heretical/ heterodox in origin; they are not secular in the sense they claim to be (free from theology), but rather are counter-theologies and quasi-theologies in disguise. Both sociology (in particular the sociology of religion) and forms of theology which have been dependent upon the "ontology of violence" at the heart of so-called secular social theories must be dismantled by orthodox Christian theology. In their place, Milbank called for a "social theology" which grows out of an "ontology of peace."

The works of Lindbeck and Milbank have contributed to shifting the conversation away from whether and how theologians can use the social sciences, toward how theologians can deeply engage with and thickly describe social groups and realities—as social scientists have done—while not accepting the premises of social sciences, but allowing the research to be shaped by theological traditions and normative concerns.

Subsequently, British theologians and theological ethicists such as Nicholas Adams and Samuel Wells have also been calling for ethnographic research methods. In an article in 2000, Adams, along with Charles Elliot, proposed wedding insights from Barth and Foucault to produce "a form of description which acknowledges the dogmatics which is at work within it, but is liberated to attend to the practices of description themselves."[7] And in his book, *Transforming Fate into Destiny*, Wells used description of the community of Le Chambon, where thousands of Jews were sheltered and rescued by Christians during World War II, to test Stanley Hauerwas's theological claims concerning community, narrative, virtue, and habit; the role of the stranger; and how nonviolence provokes a community's imagination and political activism.[8]

There is also a current movement among both British and American theologians which is advocating the use of ethnographic research in congregations for the formation of ecclesiology. Perhaps the most full-bodied and well-known argument in this conversation is Nicholas Healy's *Church, World and the Christian Life*, which argues for "ecclesiological ethnography" as a method which can help theologians overcome both the disconnected idealism and the undermining of the church's distinctiveness which Healy identifies as the twin errors of modern ecclesiology.[9]

7. Adams and Elliott, "Ethnography Is Dogmatics," 346–47.

8. Wells, *Transforming Fate into Destiny,* 134–40.

9. Other key works in this conversation include McClintock Fulkerson, *Places of Redemption*; Brown, *Converging on Culture*; and Cavanaugh, *Torture and Eucharist.*

As is perhaps already clear, most of these theologians are talking *about* doing ethnography much more than *doing* ethnography. The work which is most often cited by scholars on both sides of the Atlantic as an actual example of successful theological ethnography is William Cavanaugh's *Torture and Eucharist*, which describes the rise of Pinochet's torturing military dictatorship in Chile, how the church was at first powerless to resist the regime, and how the church eventually found its voice and the strength to stand up against torture. Just as thousands of Chileans had disappeared into the Junta's torture chambers, their bodies invisible to the world, the church had disappeared into the "spiritual" sphere, becoming invisible as a social body. According to Cavanaugh, it was through eucharistic practices that some Christians in some places and times in Chile were able to reappear as the body of Christ.

Simultaneous to the turn among these theologians toward ethnography, there have been shifts in the social sciences which perhaps make the theological employment of social-scientific methodological insights slightly less problematic than some theologians may have previously assumed. In general, the social sciences have experienced a turn away from modern, structuralist, and positivist understandings of social science and social-scientific objectivity toward post-structuralist, constructivist, and interpretivist understandings of the situatedness of the social sciences themselves as well as of the individuals who conduct social-scientific research.

One interesting outcome of this shift is the legitimization among some anthropologists of activist research. These anthropologists argue that it is not only possible, but sometimes even preferable for a social scientist who is personally dedicated to a specific cause to conduct research which aims not only to better understand the issue, but to work together with those affected by and involved in the issue to find solutions.[10]

Among anthropologists, there has also been a coming-to-grips with the postcolonial realities of their discipline. One of the widespread assumptions of early anthropologists who conducted research in those regions colonized by Europeans was that Christianity and Christian congregations were not fit subjects of study because they were nonindigenous; they were imposed upon the natives by Europeans. As colonialism began to break down, the assumption was that this imported religion would disappear. As anthropologists have had to grapple not only with the inaccuracy of this prediction, but the problematic nature of their discipline's founding

10. See, e.g., Hale, "What Is Activist Research?"

assumptions, some have come to advocate and practice the anthropology of Christianity, performing in-depth anthropological analyses of specific Christian communities.[11]

Some anthropologists of Christianity are writing ethnographies of particular congregations and Christian cultures or subcultures. One early and particularly noteworthy example of such work by an anthropologist of Christianity is Susan Friend Harding's *The Book of Jerry Falwell*, a study of Falwell and his followers as they were transformed from separatist fundamentalists into political activists in the 1980s. More recent is Joel Robbins's ethnography of the Christian culture of the Urapmin people of Papua New Guinea.[12]

Familiarity with these ethnographies should give theologians pause concerning their use of the term "ethnography." Anthropologists usually mean by the term "ethnography" something much more specific than do most theologians. An ethnography is an extraordinarily comprehensive and holistic study of a culture which usually requires several months, if not years, spent inside that culture. When theologians use the term "ethnography" to describe anything from a brief historical vignette to a theological case study, I fear we may be confusing matters more than clarifying. "Theological practices of thick description" does not roll off the tongue so easily as "ethnography," but perhaps it more accurately names what most theologians calling for and doing "theological ethnography" are actually discussing, as opposed to ethnography proper.

When theologians speak specifically of theological ethnography in relation to the study and description of particular congregations, we of course must also turn our attention toward those scholars who have been studying Christian congregations for quite some time. The discipline of congregational studies is self-consciously shaped by inheritances from anthropology, sociology, organizational studies, and theology. In the United States, the discipline has been decidedly more shaped by organizational studies, and the aims of studying a congregation are often to understand broad, institutional aspects of church life such as leadership, authority, and workflow in order to discern what is and is not "working" in a congregation and what changes need to be made. For many American practitioners of

---

11. Tim Jenkins gives a concise introduction to and overview of this field in "The Anthropology of Christianity," where he highlights the work of Fenella Cannell, Webb Keane, and Joel Robbins.

12. Robbins, *Becoming Sinners*.

congregational studies, a primary goal has been church growth. By contrast, congregational studies in the United Kingdom have been formed more by sociology and anthropology, and practitioners have often focused on congregations as social systems simply to be understood on their own terms.

In both countries, those practitioners of congregational studies who have primarily theological, instead of organizational or sociological, interests are called "practical theologians." Their work resonates more with pastoral theology than with systematics, and often begins not with a research question formed by a scholar, but with a congregational need. This type of congregational study often involves corporate approaches in which the members of the congregation actively engage in the research project and aim to make changes based on their findings. Some practical theologians more intentionally merge pastoral and systematic theology through the use of critical correlation, in which a particular theological doctrine is brought into dialogue with a contemporary congregation.[13]

It was with all this in mind that I went to visit Pastor George's church. I spent an academic term with this American Christian Zionist congregation, where I observed congregational life and conducted long, qualitative interviews. I sought to immerse myself in the pro-Israel culture of the congregation through attending worship services, Sunday School classes, prayer meetings, planning meetings, and large-scale events, reading the books that were being read and recommended by members, and exploring the Zionist organizations with which they are partners.

I was fortunate to be able to visit the congregation when their pro-Israel activism was at an annual peak. While I was there, the congregation prepared for and staged an extravagant evening program to honor Israel. Their pastor, whom everyone calls Pastor George, preached a five-week sermon series on Israel and the end times. Pastor George's wife, Cheryl, who is director of the congregation's Israel Outreach ministry, prepared a group of young singers and dancers for their departure for their annual summer tour of performances at Israeli military bases, where their goal is to communicate God's love for and blessings upon Israeli troops. A large group of delegates also prepared to join thousands of Christian Zionists to lobby the United States government through the Washington, DC, summit of Pastor John Hagee's organization, Christians United for Israel.

13. On congregational studies, see Cameron et al., *Studying Local Churches*; and Guest et al., *Congregational Studies in the UK*.

One of the main reasons I chose to study Pastor George's congregation is because they have provided support for an "adopted settlement" in the West Bank since the 1990s, and this partnership and others like it have contributed significantly to the growth and stabilization of several settlements which will almost inevitably remain in Israeli hands should a two-state solution be reached. In other words, these American Christians have been helping Israeli settlers to establish facts on the ground. I was able to visit the settlement to see the fruits of this partnership firsthand and interview the settlers about their relationships with Christian Zionists.

I arrived with pre-formed theological questions about Christian Zionist eschatology and social ethics, and with a goal in mind to make normative claims about Christian theological ethics, but I had also learned a great deal about the openness to a community's own voice which is central to the anthropologist's practice of ethnography. This resulted in research which confirmed some of my preconceptions about Christian Zionism while troubling and disconfirming many others.

I concluded that the deeply problematic eschatology of Christian Zionism so alters their Christology and ecclesiology as to disconnect them from the Christological and ecclesiological resources which are necessary for well-formed Christian social ethics. I may have been able to reach that conclusion through textual research alone. However, my further conclusion, which was entirely unexpected and which I feel sure I could not have reached without spending time with the congregation, listening to and observing the enactment of their theopolitical discourse, is that their understanding of how eschatology relates to social ethics was surprisingly persuasive and even convicting.

Contrary to popular stereotypes which portray Christian Zionists as believing they can make Jesus return sooner through their pro-Israel activism, I found this congregation had rightly discerned that eschatology is not only a chronology of end-times events, but is also a doctrine of God's intentions for humanity and all creation, and of the status of those intentions in the time between the two advents of Jesus Christ. They believe they are engaging in the discernment of God's ultimate intentions for creation, discernment of God's ways of enacting these intentions in the world, and discernment of how they should best cooperate with God through participation in those purposes and those ways. I do not believe I could have been open to the complexity or the virtues of this understanding if I had not listened to and observed its enactment in person.

In my day-to-day interactions with Pastor George's congregation, there were long spans of time during which I was experiencing the lives of entirely average, middle-class Americans in an entirely mainstream evangelical megachurch. There were moments of sympathy and appreciation, moments of friendship and warmth. And there were moments of repugnance, shock, and dismay at certain beliefs, comments, and practices. This is the ambivalent reality of the human condition which is only fully experienced by entering into people's lives. I was not fully prepared for this ambivalence, and I quickly realized that I would not have been able to take Christian Zionists truly seriously as fellow Christians if my research had been only textual. This also taught me that the theologians practicing "ethnography" must take the complexity of human beings seriously enough neither to overstate the negative aspects of congregations which are deemed misguided in theology and ethics, nor to understate the negative aspects of congregations which are deemed exemplary.

Theologians, and I would argue theological ethicists in particular, should intentionally and carefully attend to the complex realities of the actual people involved in the compelling theological and social issues of our day. Genuine attentiveness to people and genuine engagement with the complexities of their lives is only possible through research methods which take theologians beyond the desk and the library and into those lives. As we continue to discuss, explore, and develop such methods, we must be serious apprentices of sociologists, anthropologists, philosophers, and historians— all those who have long grappled with questions of how best to attend to the complexities of the human condition. However, in our apprenticeship to other disciplines, we must not lose sight of the crucial distinction that our task is first and foremost theological.

In one sense, I am only saying what has already been said by many Christian ethicists in the last few decades: that it is in no way helpful to preserve the old distinction between theological ethics and social ethics, which has followed modern scientific distinctions between so-called pure and applied research. However, I hope I am also saying more than this— more than just that Christian ethicists are theologians, not social scientists, and yet theologians should not be entirely dismissive of what we can learn from the social sciences. I am suggesting that more theologians who are writing on war and peace should spend time in war zones, with victims of war, with soldiers, with peacemakers. More theologians who are writing on the environment should visit sites of particular environmental concern;

environmentalist groups, anti-environmentalist activists. And more theologians should spend time deeply engaging with the lives of particular Christian congregations.

As those who claim to be reflecting on the Christian life, theological ethicists in particular must seriously consider more frequent employment of research methods which involve encounter with actual Christians in the communities in which they are seeking to live the Christian life. These may be entirely average congregations, or particularly exemplary congregations, or (as in the case of my own research) congregations engaged in practices which the ethicist finds particularly problematic. For all those Christian ethicists who identify to any degree with the ecclesiological and ethnographic turns which theology and ethics have taken in the last few decades, the study of particular congregations should be a clear and pressing consideration in the formulation of research projects.

For all Christians studying congregations, attention to the complex admixture of faithful and flawed convictions and practices in other individuals and congregations can also helpfully draw attention to one's own unexamined assumptions, beliefs, and practices. This dynamic takes on a unique and important function when congregational research is done by a theologian for theological purposes—namely, that God is a recognized actor in the analytical process. The theologian can encounter the congregation not as subjects pinned under a microscope, but as persons held before God. And when persons are held before God that we might understand them better, their peculiarities for good or ill become prisms through which God's light allows us to see ourselves and our own peculiarities more clearly. When we enter into the lives of those we are researching, we must observe and question and listen as theologians. We are not scientists, and human beings are not our subjects. We are theologians, and we enter into the lives and struggles of fellow human beings because we need to hold them before God and for God to hold them before us so that we can see them as they are, and allow them to help us see ourselves anew for what we are.

CHAPTER 6

Saying "Peace" When There Is No Peace: An American Christian Zionist Congregation on Peace, Militarism, and Settlements (2014)

In a typical Colorado suburb, a skywalk stretches over a major thorough-fare connecting a 1970s church building with the congregation's larger and newer facilities (the Family Worship Center) on the other side of the road. At a corner facing a busy intersection, letters five feet tall spell the church's name (which the members shorten to FBC) and water cascades over them into a fountain below. Large electronic signs face both directions, flashing service times and upcoming events to motorists waiting at the traffic signal.

On Sunday mornings, nearly four thousand people congregate at FBC, and there are at least four police officers directing traffic around the church building. After being directed to a parking space, members walk to the Family Worship Center along paths lined with speakers amplifying praise music. Just outside the main entrance is a large, golden sculpture of a globe, which appears to be lifted up by the water of the fountain below it. At every door members greet those arriving. Inside the main entrance is a cavernous lobby with floor-to-ceiling windows and flags of the countries of the world suspended from white metal support beams that span the ceiling high above the entering worshipers. Some move straight through toward the sanctuary, others stop to peruse the various stalls of merchandise, and others buy a cup of espresso at the café.

Praying for the Peace of Jerusalem

On one wall there is a large depiction of a Jewish man blowing a shofar between two mountains and two tablets with Hebrew writing. The image is surrounded by the inscription: "Let the sound of the shofar bind the majestic mountains of Colorado with the holy mountains of Judea and bring unity of Christian and Jew." Next to another wall composed of large white stones, a plaque reads, "This wall is made of Jerusalem stone and stands as a reminder of God's covenant promises to Israel." Across the Jerusalem stones are the words "Pray for the Peace of Jerusalem" written in large black metal letters. Many members take these words very seriously.

Members of FBC are encouraged to pray regularly for Israel, and many corporate gatherings include such prayers. Adjacent to the Family Worship Center is the freestanding Prayer Chapel. Inside, about forty seats face a small dais, flanked by American and Israeli flags. The walls of the small chapel are lined with prayer stations with large bulletin boards that have requests and guidance for prayer, each with a heading: "Our Church," "Missions," "Nations," "Urgent Needs," "Personal Requests," and "Israel." The Israel station encourages prayers for the safety and blessing of Israelis, increased immigration of Jews into Israel, a stronger Israeli economy, the rounding up and punishment of "anti-Israel world leaders and terrorists," the establishment of "biblical and secure" borders, and wisdom for Israel's leaders. Below these prayer requests and the accompanying Scriptures, photographs, and documents displayed with them, there sits a box of tissues for the use of those weeping in prayer.

One night each month, about twenty members of FBC meet in the prayer chapel to intercede on Israel's behalf. They are led in prayer by Cheryl, Pastor George's wife, who is on staff full time in charge of the Israel Outreach Ministry and the Women's Ministry. I happened to arrive at FBC on the day of the monthly Israel prayer meeting, and this was my first introduction to the congregation.[1] When Cheryl arrived in the prayer chapel, she moved the chairs into a large circle. She prayed under her breath as she arranged the room, saying, "Yes, Jesus. Thank you, Jesus." The chairs in the circle were soon filled and Cheryl led the group in prayer. She told them that she had seen an article on the *Jerusalem Post* website reporting a military buildup on Israel's border with Syria. She explained that this was

---

1. I first arrived at FBC in May 2007.

significant because there was a prophecy "among the believers"[2] in Israel that there would be a war with Syria soon, and she had personally received a word from God while in the Golan Heights several years earlier regarding coming war with Syria.

The group received this news as their marching orders for the prayer meeting, but to my surprise no one prayed for an easing of tensions between Israel and Syria; no one prayed for the military buildup to end; no one prayed that there would not be war. One man prayed, "We hope there does not have to be a war. But we know that your word says that wars are coming." They prayed that the war would happen in God's good time, and that the Israeli military would be prepared and not fail as they had in Lebanon in 2006. They prayed that Jewish casualties would be minimal. They prayed that the US government would support Israel and not stand in the way of whatever Israel needed to do, and that God would turn the president's heart against the "road map" to peace. One man prayed, "We don't want a road map to peace." They prayed that no one would seek to restrain Israel's military, and that America would supply whatever weapons Israel needed. They prayed for Israel to be empowered to wipe out their enemies, "because they are your enemies, God." Cheryl prayed fervently for fatality among Israel's enemies. She said, "Let Syria make a fatal mistake, Lord. Let Hezbollah make a fatal mistake. Let Hamas make a fatal mistake. Let Iran make a fatal mistake." At the end of the hour, everyone in the circle stood, joined hands, and sang together, "Lord we bless, Lord we love thy people. Lord we bless, Lord we love thy land. We weep for, we pray for, intercede for Israel. Lord, now move thy hand."

I walked away from this prayer meeting stunned by the force with which people had prayed for violence and death. I realized that I had a lot to learn about how these average middle-class American evangelicals could reconcile what they were praying with the idea of praying for peace.

STUDYING CHRISTIAN ZIONISM

I spent six weeks at FBC observing their congregational life and conducting interviews.[3] I read the books they read, listened to the prophecy teachers they trust, and explored the organizations they support. When I told

2. A phrase used by some Christian Zionists to describe Jews who have been converted to Christianity.

3. May–June 2007.

friends that I was doing this research, many replied, "Oh, those are the people who think they can make Jesus return sooner by supporting Israel!" Before this project began, I had shared this assumption; I was sure one outcome of my research would be a critique of the belief that political activism can hasten the second coming.[4] I found instead what we always find when we attend to the convictions and lives of real people: that it is much more complicated. In fact, though my experiences with Christian Zionists and their Israeli partners were no less disturbing than I expected, they were far more compelling than I could have imagined.

Much of the literature on Christian Zionism is written as exposé, to convince us that Christian Zionism is politically dangerous or biblically unsound. Descriptions of the battle of Armageddon figure prominently in these portrayals, and "Armageddon" often finds its way into their titles.[5] While I share these authors' concerns, I also wanted to move beyond exposé and get to know particular Zionist Christians—to take their complexity seriously. I did not find that the people at FBC have a fanatical thirst for the bloodshed of Armageddon; instead they have an utter certitude that they are cooperating with God in the fruition of God's ultimate intentions for human history. Pastor George summarized this well in a sermon on Ezekiel's vision of the dry bones,[6] which he and many Christian Zionists interpret as a prophecy of the modern State of Israel. Pastor George drew the congregation's attention to the verse in which God tells Ezekiel to prophesy to the bones (Ezek 37:3). When Ezekiel did this, the bones took on flesh and became living bodies, which is interpreted as a prediction of the return of Jews to Palestine and Israeli statehood. Pastor George related this passage to FBC's support of Israel today. He said, "God called Ezekiel into partnership to prophesy to the bones. God wants us to cooperate with his purposes. That's what we're doing . . . we're cooperating with God and we're speaking life into this situation."

4. It has long been of interest to me that differing forms of this conviction have been central to both conservative and liberal activist movements within American Christianity. While both historical and theological literature tend to view postmillennial and premillennial movements as opposites, it is also the case that certain forms of these eschatologies have been two sides of the same coin of confidence in the relationship between human activism and the millennium.

5. See, for example, Clark, *Allies for Armageddon*; Cohn-Sherbok, *Politics of Apocalypse*; Sizer, *Christian Zionism: Road-Map to Armageddon?*; Wagner, *Anxious for Armageddon*.

6. May 20, 2007.

This conviction about cooperating with God's purposes, and the activism through which the people of FBC believe they are enacting such cooperation, are complex realities. Through the following portraits of FBC's support for Israel, I hope to offer a glimpse into the complexity involved in both their theology and their activism and demonstrate that there are serious problems to confront, but also interesting lessons to learn.

ISRAEL AS BLESSING

FBC began as a small group of families meeting in homes in the mid-1960s. Most of these families had moved to Colorado from California for the purpose of planting a new church. Their efforts began with Bible studies in one another's homes, and much of their Bible study was focused on prophecies concerning Israel—a central concern of the congregation from its inception. According to members, a leader of the congregation in California received a prophetic word that God wanted the new church to "bless his people." This word was not understood until the pastor began studying his Bible in order to decipher the message and determined that Genesis 12:3 was the key.

As with many Christian Zionists, Genesis 12:3 became central for the fledgling FBC. It is part of the narrative of God's promise to Abram, in which God says to Abram, "I will bless those who bless you, and the one who curses you I will curse; and in you all the families of the earth shall be blessed."

In 1973, members of the church began touring Israel together. On their first tour, the group visited the Golan Heights (the land at the northern tip of Israel that was seized from Syria in the 1967 war). As they stood on top of a former Syrian bunker overlooking the surrounding hills and a kibbutz in the valley below, their Israeli tour guide described the 1967 conflict to them. He told them that when the question arose whether or not to take the Golan, they felt like they had to do it "for the children." He explained that before the Golan was taken, the children in this kibbutz did not know the difference between the sound of thunder and the sound of mortar fire.

The group was deeply moved by his version of the events of 1967. One of the men said, "I just feel we need to do what Genesis 12:3 says, that we need to stand here and bless Israel from this place that it's been cursed from for so many years," and they began to pray and to bless Israel. There was a young newlywed couple with that 1973 tour group who are both full-time members of the church's ministerial staff today. She often tells the story of what happened next on that day in the Golan—and she cries every time: "As we turned to leave, it was just like heaven opened, and I just heard this simple song, 'I will bless those who bless my people. I will curse those who curse them too. For this I have promised to my servant Abraham. I will keep my word.'" She sang the song for the group there on the Golan Heights and they were overcome. The song is still sung at nearly every Israel-related event at the church, and this is the song they sang at the end of the prayer meeting I attended when I first arrived at FBC.

This narrative is at the very heart of the congregation's self-understanding, and their interpretation of the Genesis passage is at the very heart of their understanding of God's purposes in the world. They believe that God created a people—Israel—to bless and to make a blessing to the rest of the world. They believe that throughout history, when an empire has cursed Jews, God has cursed that empire. Every anti-Jewish, anti-Israel empire has fallen, from ancient Rome to medieval Spain to modern Germany and Britain. They believe this will be the fate of America as well if the people do not bless Israel in every way possible. However, if America cooperates with God in blessing Israel, America will not only be blessed, but will also see Israel become a blessing to all nations. Along with many Christian Zionists, the members of FBC have an eschatological vision influenced by dispensational premillennialism. They believe that after the chaos, violence, and suffering of the great tribulation at the end of this present age, the Messiah will return, all surviving Jews will accept him as Lord and King, and he will set up the millennial kingdom, ruling the earth from its capital in Jerusalem. Out of Israel there will radiate a one-thousand-year era of uninterrupted and incorruptible peace and prosperity over all the earth.

This is the congregation's vision of God's intentions for humanity; these are the purposes of God with which they believe they are cooperating. In this sense, they believe that a prayer for Israel is always a prayer for peace. However, they also believe that there will be a lot of conflict and violence between now and that coming age of peace, and as far as they are concerned, cooperating with God's purposes means cooperating in the militarism and occupation that will precede the millennium. They believe in helping God's chosen people execute violence instead of suffering violence at the hands of others. For this reason, one of the primary ways they seek to participate in the realities of the coming of the millennium is through support for the Israeli military.

BLESSING THE ISRAELI DEFENSE FORCES

Over three decades ago, FBC began sending a performance group on summer tours of Israeli military bases. While the style and content of their performances has changed over the years, the message has remained the same: they want Israeli soldiers to know that there are Christians who bless and support them, and who believe they are acting as God's chosen people. Today, the group is called the Internationals, and being a member of this group requires nearly year-round study and rehearsals. Often FBC members become interested in joining The Internationals because their parents or friends have been members. Some begin dancing with the children's group, the Little Internationals, and grow up wanting to become Internationals. Others join the group to make friends, for the opportunity to perform, or because they have been recruited, and only after joining do they come to understand the group's mission. Internationals are not only trained in singing and dancing—including coaching from Israeli consultants on choreography and pronunciation of Hebrew lyrics—they are also given lectures and assignments on Israel, including readings such as "Why Christians Should Support Israel," by John Hagee.

When I met the Internationals, they were five singers in their thirties and forties, and twelve dancers ranging in age from sixteen to twenty-two. On their approximately eighteen-day tour, the Internationals perform at about thirteen locations, most of which are military bases. Each performance includes about a dozen numbers, and there is a costume change between every one. These range from black satin Haredi Jewish costumes, which the male dancers wear for a folk dance, to Orthodox Jewish wedding clothes for a dance to "L'Haim," to fluorescent T-shirts and Capri pants for a modern Israeli pop number, to Israeli military uniforms for a tribute number.

One dancer reflected on the significance of performing for the military. She said the military was "the core of Israel's being." Another remarked how moved she was by the differing life situations of teens in American and Israel: "We're about to go off to college, and they're about to go fight for their country." Cheryl leads the tour each year, and she warns the group in advance that their schedule will be grueling. "And I'll be yelling at you, telling you to do this and that, and if that offends you, you need to get over it. If you need to be treated like a little kid, get plenty of that from your momma before we leave!"

The people of FBC think of Israel as a fundamentally dangerous place, and the performers go on tour with a sense that it may cost them their lives. One young teenager told me he thought they would be safe due to God's protection; "But if we're not," he said, "I'm ready to go." A staff member who had participated in multiple tours and was preparing to tour again along with her daughter and son-in-law (who prepared for the tour by drafting a new will naming the legal guardian of their two-year-old twins) told me without hesitation, "If we don't come home, we don't come home, and it will have been worth it."

Another woman who had gone on tour as a chaperone along with her teenage son became emotional when she described why FBC considers the tour to be worth this level of risk:

> The thing that really was amazing to me was watching these average kids, you know, these kids that I know . . . and they go there and they bless these soldiers who are defending this land . . . just these average, middle-class, Christian kids blessing the apple of God's eye, you know? Defending the land that God gave them.

The members of FBC believe that the Israeli military is acting in accordance with God's will—even more than that, they are the foretaste and herald of the ultimate military victory of all time, which they believe will occur at Jesus's second coming. When he returns, it will be to vanquish Israel's enemies and to bring Israel into her rightful place: the center of history, politics, religion, and culture. These Christian Zionists do not believe their support of Israel will persuade Jesus to come back any sooner or make him any more successful when he arrives. They do believe they are cooperating with and participating in the future military victory that they believe is sure.

BLESSING THE SETTLEMENTS

Along with this vision of Israeli soldiers as forerunners of the coming divine military victory, FBC sees Israeli settlers in the occupied territories as pioneers on the divine frontier. Thus, FBC not only supports the Israeli military, they also have an "adopted settlement" in the West Bank. The settlement of Ariel had its humble beginning in 1978, when a young Israeli named Ron Nachman led a small group of settlers who flew in by helicopter to a West Bank hilltop and slept in tents until buildings were erected. The settlement grew quickly, and in the 1990s it was adopted by the congregation at FBC. Today, Ariel is no longer a humble outpost; it is a city with over 19,000 residents. Nachman was elected as the first mayor when the outpost became a city, and he was repeatedly re-elected, serving as mayor until his death in January 2013.

The youth of Ariel can receive their entire education inside the settlement. There are multiple preschools, elementary schools, and junior high schools, one high school, and a college.[7] There is a shopping center, three medical clinics, a large public swimming pool, an extensive central park, a cultural center, a sports complex, and over one hundred small plants and factories.

Ariel is a city surrounded by a bloc of smaller settlements, all of which are known as "consensus communities"—settlements inside the Palestinian territories that Israel has determined, with the support of American leaders, will remain Israeli in any future agreement with a Palestinian state. This "consensus" status makes Ariel a particularly strategic partner for Christian Zionists, and also makes their partnership especially controversial. Ariel is situated east of the strip of Israel that would be extremely thin—just nine miles wide at some points—if the Green Line[8] became the Israel-Palestine border. Inclusion of the Ariel bloc would more than double the width of this strip of land, as Ariel is located twelve miles to the east of the Green Line. Prime Ministers Ariel Sharon, Ehud Olmert, and Benjamin Netanyahu have all committed publicly to annex the Ariel bloc into Israel proper. Netanyahu visited Ariel in 2010, proclaiming it the "capital of Samaria" and an "integral part of Israel."[9] The likelihood of annexation seems confirmed by the path of the Israeli "security fence" (which Palestinians call "the wall"); it dips deep inside the West Bank to surround Ariel. During his time as mayor, Nachman often quipped, "I don't call it a wall or a fence. I call it a gated community."[10]

7. Controversially, the college was renamed "Ariel University Center of Samaria" in 2005 in an attempt to claim for itself the status of university, which most government officials were unwilling to grant to a college in a settlement. University status was officially granted in 2012. See Paraszczuk, "Ariel Gets University Status Despite Opposition."

8. The Green Line is the border between Israel and the Palestinian territories drawn in the 1949 Armistice Agreement.

9. Lazaroff, "PM: Ariel Is the 'Capital of Samaria.'"

10. All quotations from Nachman and other residents of Ariel, unless otherwise noted, are from interviews I conducted in Ariel, September 2007.

For most of its history, Ariel has maintained close connections with and benefited from the financial assistance of evangelical Christians. Ron Nachman and Dina Shalit, director of the Ariel Development Fund, have cultivated friendships with many Christian Zionist groups, from whom Ariel receives an average of fifteen visits per year. Nachman and Shalit were often guests at Nights to Honor Israel at American churches. Another of Nachman's characteristic quips was his statement of preference for speaking in churches rather than synagogues when visiting America. "When I visit synagogues, I get a lot of questions," he said, "but when I visit churches, I get big checks."

When I visited Ariel, I was often told that the main impact of Christian support for the settlement was the improvement of the settlers' quality of life. The funds and services provided by groups such as FBC have made Ariel feel like a genuine city instead of an outpost. In fact, Ariel now feels much more like a suburb of Tel Aviv than a radical base of occupation. FBC's role in this transformation includes donations of an ark for Torah scrolls, medical and educational supplies and equipment, college scholarships, and financial support for development projects ranging from a Holocaust museum to improved soldiers' quarters. They are particularly proud of their endowment of Ariel's Child Development Center, a facility for speech, occupational, psychological, and physical therapies, as well as tutoring for children with learning disabilities. Cheryl remembers,

> When we adopted Ariel, we asked the Lord, "What do you want us to do there?" And the Scripture came to me when Jesus said, "When you've done it to the least of these my brethren, you've done it to me." So we said, "Who would be the least in Ariel?" And it would be the children who have emotional, physical, and learning disabilities.

Mearsheimer and Walt, in their controversial book on the "Israel lobby," argue that the efforts of Christian Zionist groups to support Israeli settlements have made a significant difference in Middle East politics. They cite FBC as a "celebrated example" of this impact. "Absent their support, settlers would be less numerous in Israel, and the US and Israeli government would be less constrained by their presence in the Occupied Territories as well as their political activities."[11] One of the deeply problematic aspects of this sort of support for settlements has been highlighted in the *New York Times*, which reported, "As the American government seeks to

11. Mearsheimer and Walt, *Israel Lobby and US Foreign Policy*, 138.

end the four-decade Jewish settlement enterprise and foster a Palestinian state in the West Bank, the American Treasury helps sustain the settlements through tax breaks on donations to support them." Even though the United States will not allow American aid money to be spent on settlements, at least forty groups in America, like FBC, currently raise funds for settlements through tax-deductible donations.[12]

Ariel's partnership with FBC has also resulted in a performance group called For Zion's Sake. Inspired by the Internationals, these Israeli teenagers tour America, performing mainly for Christian Zionists, thanking them for their support and soliciting further donations. At one performance, the teens went offstage to change into cowboy and cowgirl costumes, and Dina Shalit introduced their "Western dance" number by drawing an analogy between the American West and the Israeli West Bank: "In the US, it was settlers who built the country, spreading the borders past the original thirteen colonies. Your history, however, only reflects admiration for the settlers." By contrast, according to Shalit and many of the settlers I interviewed, Israeli settlers are scorned by international critics and fellow Israelis alike, who consider them to be dangerous extremists.

Youth workers in the settlement told me that this treatment leaves the Israeli teens of the West Bank feeling isolated and rejected, which often results in their rejection of Judaism and the settlement project. However, for some of these teens, a sort of conversion occurs when Christian Zionists reach out to them with stirring messages of God's purposes for Israel and the Israeli right to the occupied territories. This has led some teens to recommit to Jewish faith, to their role in the Israeli military, and to the importance of the settlements. These relationships between young Christians and young settlers are cultivating both future American supporters of Israel's claims to land in the West Bank and future Israeli defenders and expanders of the settlements.

An important chapter of Ariel's story was missing from all these conversations. Neither the members of FBC nor the people I interviewed in Ariel cared to acknowledge the darkest side of Ariel: the impact of the settlement on Palestinians in surrounding villages. According to Robert Friedman, a journalist who researched extremism among Israeli settlers, during the first intifada settlers in Ariel formed a covert, armed militia under the leadership of Ron Nachman, with weapons provided by the

---

12. Rutenberg, McIntire, and Bronner, "Tax Exempt Funds Aid Settlements in West Bank."

Israeli military. Friedman chronicled attacks carried out by Ariel's militia, including invasions of Palestinian homes, beatings, fatal shootings of both militants and innocent children, and burning of agricultural fields and olive groves.[13] Friedman also reported that as a member of the Knesset, Ron Nachman proposed that Arabs working in settlements should be required to wear yellow "alien worker" tags.

CONCLUSION

How, then, do the members of FBC reconcile praying for peace with supporting militarism and a settlement that hinders the peace process and condones violence against its Palestinian neighbors? In the theopolitical imagination of this Christian Zionist congregation, the Israeli military functions as a forerunner of the ultimate Israeli military victory to come, and Israeli settlers function as pioneers on the frontiers of prophetic fulfillment. They believe that through their support of the military and the settlers, they are cooperating with God in the fulfillment of God's purposes and the coming of God's peace.

Many critics of Christian Zionism, both journalistic and scholarly, insist that this is the sort of misguided politics that results from the influence of eschatology. They argue that politics arising from convictions about the "end times" are inevitably dangerous. Other scholars suggest that eschatology has little or nothing to do with the core of Christian Zionist convictions and politics. We have been needlessly distracted by apocalyptic rhetoric, they argue.

I found among the particular Christian Zionist community at FBC that eschatology was in fact at the core of their theopolitics. I would argue that problems do not arise because of the interrelation between their eschatology and their politics *per se*, nor because they do not understand how best to relate eschatology to politics. Although the particular eschatology at the root of their Zionism is deeply problematic, and their politics are equally problematic, I found that the people of FBC do have an understanding of the relationship between eschatology and politics, and an amazing will to act on the implications of that relationship, which is surprisingly persuasive.

13. Friedman, "Settlers," and "West Bank Story," in which Dina Shalit of Ariel's mayor's office refutes Friedman's claims and Friedman responds.

Christian Zionists are well known for their affinity for the end-time scenarios predicted by dispensational premillennialism. Their critics often portray them as people obsessed with this chronology, whether portrayed in the detailed charts of the dispensations from the Scofield Reference Bible or the more recent, action-packed novels and films from the *Left Behind* series. My findings at FBC—where, to be sure, these charts and novels have figured prominently in the past—were surprisingly different. These particular Christians have rightly discerned that eschatology is not only a chronology of end-times events; it is also a doctrine of God's intentions for humanity and all creation, and of the status of those intentions in the time between the two advents of Jesus Christ.

Even though they would not articulate it this way, I think they have rightly concluded that politics should be formed by eschatology through discernment of God's ultimate intentions for creation, of God's ways of enacting these intentions in the world, and of how Christians can cooperate with God through participation in those purposes and those ways. Their vision of a coming age of peace is a particular version of a conviction all Christians share; it is the hope of the redemption of all creation, which is central to Christian eschatology.

Yet their discernment of God's ways of inaugurating this age—through militaristic and nationalist violence and domination—are considerably more problematic, and allow them to find ethical normativity in present-day militarism and occupation. Tragically, interpretation of biblical texts as literal predictions and descriptions of the unfolding of God's nationalist and militaristic intentions obscures Scripture's own critiques of militarism, nationalism, violence, and injustice—even though these critiques are often strongest in the apocalyptic and prophetic texts that are given so much attention by Christian Zionists.

CHAPTER 7

Against Anxiety, Beyond Triumphalism:
An Eastertide Sermon (2009)

This evening I will engage in what is surely becoming an honored, if recent, Anglican tradition: borrowing a little something from the work of Rowan Williams. He once gave an address on Christian mission and spirituality, which has been published under the title "Against Anxiety, Beyond Triumphalism."[1] Though his address was on an entirely different topic, and he used the two phrases quite differently than I will here, I would like to borrow his title and expand upon it to answer the question posed by this term's theme for Sunday Evensong: What does the resurrection faith mean to and for me? Because I believe the centuries-old faith of the church in the resurrection of our Lord stands against anxiety while also drawing us beyond triumphalism.

Let me first consider the resurrection against anxiety. In the Gospel accounts of Mark and Matthew, the women who go to Jesus's tomb are met by an angel who says to them, "Do not be afraid." In Matthew's Gospel, the women are also met by Jesus himself, who also says, "Do not be afraid." Luke recounts the resurrected Jesus coming to the gathered disciples, saying, "Peace be with you, . . . Why are you frightened, and why do doubts arise in your hearts?"

1. In Williams, *Ray of Darkness.*

Jesus's followers were, of course, afraid because they found themselves facing an empty tomb and the appearance of the living man whose dead body they expected to be lying in that tomb. Jesus and the angels said "Do not be afraid" to them for those very specific reasons. But the resurrection of Christ also speaks the words "Do not be afraid" far beyond that small circle of awestruck and frightened women and men to whom he first appeared. The resurrected Christ continues to speak through the ages: "Do not be afraid," my promises are true. "Do not be afraid," I have not left you to ruin. "Do not be afraid," I am with you. "Do not be afraid," death is not the final word.

This is more than a divinely therapeutic "There, there. Don't worry, love." This "Do not be afraid" is a call to look the resurrected Lord full in the face, to behold his power and victory and glory, and to rest in it. Rest in the assurance that no amount of work or striving or planning or anxious worrying on our part can do anything like the saving, transformational work that was done on Easter morning.

In the past two years, a strong word against anxiety has been pressed upon me in the season of Lent, leading into Easter. I have found myself in moments of profound realization of the simplest truth, one which I suspect I will spend a lifetime trying to fully grasp. That is, that one of the most fundamental implications of our Lenten meditations upon our own mortality and creatureliness, and our Easter celebrations of the resurrection power of our Creator God, is this: I am not in control, and that is a good thing.

For some of you, this may be an entirely straightforward statement which you can readily embrace. For others of us, it is a fierce challenge. I am all too aware of the fact that I am a control freak. All I really want in life is to be told exactly what is expected, what is to be done, and I will do it and thereby control the outcome of all the various dimensions of my life. Unsurprisingly, life increasingly frustrates this simple plan, presenting me with situations of stress, loss, disappointment, and uncertainty over which I have absolutely no control. No one can give me a set of instructions for reaching a solution, and nothing I do can determine the outcome.

When I find myself the most angry, the most depressed, the most out of control, is when I am in fact *out of control*, when life refuses to follow my simple just-tell-me-how-to-make-this-come-out-right plan. Meditations in Lent upon mortality, frailty, imperfection—all the attributes and behaviors which result from the fact that I am creature and not Creator—combined with celebrations in Easter of the resurrection power of our Creator God, draw me toward the inescapable conclusion that it is rather a good thing that I am not in control. And then I find myself wondering, why on earth did I ever want to be in control when I can rest in the assurance that this mighty, creating, loving, resurrecting God is in control? In these moments, I taste the profound power of the resurrection against anxiety, and the Lord speaks a tender, Easter-morning "Do not be afraid."

Unfortunately, these are only moments, and they pass, and anxiety creeps back in, and I want to be in control again. The desire to be in control is manifested in many different ways in different people's lives. This is a huge spectrum which ranges all the way from people who actually seize control of societies and bodies so that they can dominate them, to people who control their loved ones through criticism and demands, to people who descend into eating disorders because their food intake is the only thing they feel they can truly control. I suspect that many of us will spend our whole lives relearning this lesson and renewing our non-anxious rest in God. And I am thankful that for all of us control freaks, Lent and Easter return every year and will continue to speak to us God's word against anxiety, to press us to embrace the very basic fact that we are not in control, and that is a good thing.

And yet, while the resurrection speaks this clear word against anxiety, it also draws us beyond triumphalism. One might wonder, what could be more triumphant than resurrection from the dead? What faith could claim to be more triumphant than that which is centered upon this stunning victory over death? But the very nature of the resurrection itself calls us to renounce all pretences to power and superiority over others. This is one of the profound surprises of Easter which many of us have not yet grasped.

Easter, like the spring season in which we celebrate it, is full of surprises. Having lived in Southern California for several years before coming to England, I find myself completely fascinated with the rhythm of the changing British seasons. I know some of you are sure to have little sympathy with what I am about to say, but I feel something very important was lost living in a place where it is warm enough to eat dinner outside all year round and where things are perpetually in blossom and bloom. This is my fourth year in Cambridge, and I am still entirely surprised by the experience of spring here. I am surprised how much better I feel when the days grow longer, how much the flowers along the backs of the colleges change from week to week, how irresistibly adorable ducklings are, how entertaining it is to wait for the family of pheasants in Jesus College to appear with their newborns, how ecstatic I feel when I see new blossoms and smell new scents, and get to pack away my boots and bring out the sandals. Spring feels like a wonderland of surprises.

Easter is full of surprises as well, but much more unexpected surprises than those of the changing seasons. Not only is there the obvious, but ever-challenging surprise of a dead man who is suddenly living, walking, and eating with his friends; there is the further, quite unexpected fact that this miraculously risen god-man is wounded. His resurrected body is not a body free from the marks of the torments inflicted upon him. And while I am sure many a skeptic has been dissuaded from the Christian faith by the utter improbability and unbelievability of resurrection from the dead, I will tell you what I find even more improbable and unbelievable: that human beings would have imagined for themselves a religion in which God performs such a miraculously powerful deed and yet presents us with a resurrection body which is not perfect and without flaw or evidence of brokenness, but is scarred, wounded, indelibly marked.

When the resurrected Jesus came and stood in the midst of his gathered disciples, he was not what we might consider a vision of heavenly perfection. There were unhealed wounds where nails had been driven through his body. There was an unhealed incision in his side where he had been pierced with a spear. When his disciples doubted that it was truly him, or took him to be a ghost, he invited them to see and feel his very evident wounds. Now, of course, for the Gospel writers, the primary function of describing these wounds was to make the very important point that this was a bodily resurrection; that the disciples saw a living, breathing, eating man, and not a vision or a spirit. But just as the words "Do not be afraid" speak to us as well as to the women at the empty tomb, so do the words "Look at my hands and my feet" speak to us as well as to the bewildered disciples.

And this is where the resurrection draws us beyond triumphalism. There is something deep within humanity which longs for God to triumph on our terms, the way we would triumph over others if we were all-powerful. We want Jesus to be the comic book hero who rises from what seemed utter defeat at the hands of his enemies and overcomes them in a blaze of violent triumph. The disciples wanted that on Good Friday; when Jesus went to the garden to pray, they went ready for a fight with the Romans. And Christians throughout the centuries have wanted it as well, convinced that even though Jesus did not quite get around to crushing his enemies the first time because of all of that pesky cross business, he is sure to return and do it in the end.

For the past few years I have been studying a group of Christians with a very particular form of triumphalist faith, American Christian Zionism. These Christians take literally certain portions of the prophetic books of the Hebrew Scriptures and the book of Revelation which describe fierce battles preceding an age of peace and prosperity. They believe that Jesus will return at the end of history as a military victor, intervening in a global war to defeat his enemies and establish his empire on earth. And they believe that resurrected Christians will be soldiers in this end-time army, dealing out death and destruction to everyone who does not recognize Jesus as Messiah and Lord. I once heard one of their favorite television preachers say, only half jokingly, "Whenever I visit Jerusalem, I like to try and spot the land I want to conquer!" When Christians of this sort meet together, they often rehearse this rallying cry: the preacher says, referring to Revelation, the last book of the Bible, "I've read the end of the book, and guess what happens?" and all the congregation shouts in reply, "We win!"

They have forgotten a very important dimension of the book of Revelation, one which perhaps you and I forget as well, even if not in such stark terms. That is, in the reading we heard earlier (Revelation 5), when the heavenly elders in John's vision tell him to look and see the mighty, triumphant lion who has conquered, John turns and sees a lamb which has been slaughtered and yet lives. And all the heavenly creatures worship the slain lamb, singing that the lamb is worthy because he was slaughtered.

The cross of Jesus Christ was not a pesky business he had to get out of the way so that he could get on to the resurrection and his own ultimate triumph. His suffering was not a mistake which was corrected by the resurrection. He was not raised up and glorified in spite of his wounds and his suffering, but because of them. As we read in the Christ hymn in the letter to the Philippians, Jesus

> emptied himself, taking the form of a slave, being born in human likeness. And being found in human form, he humbled himself and became obedient to the point of death—even death on a cross. Therefore God also highly exalted him and gave him the name that is above every name, so that at the name of Jesus every knee should bend, in heaven and on earth and under the earth, and every tongue should confess that Jesus Christ is Lord, to the glory of God the Father. (Phil 2:7–11 NRSV)

The resurrection and exaltation of Jesus Christ are not compensation for or correction of his cross, but the fulfillment of his cross. They are a stamp upon the passion of Christ which reads, "Such are my triumphant ways in the world." God does not triumph as you and I would if we were all-powerful, nor does God triumph the way we might, in our heart of hearts, desire an all-powerful God to triumph on our behalf. Jesus triumphs through suffering service. He is raised up through humility and humiliation. And just as the resurrection is not a correction of the cross, neither will be Jesus's second coming. For just as the resurrected Jesus came to his frightened disciples with open wounds, so he will return in glory. Yes, a triumphant, conquering lion, but one who comes as a slaughtered lamb. Just as it says in the Charles Wesley hymn, "Lo! He Comes with Clouds Descending":

> Those dear tokens of his passion
> Still his dazzling body bears;
> Cause of endless exultation
> To his ransomed worshippers;
> With what rapture, with what rapture
> Gaze we on those glorious scars!

The risen Lord stands before us and says, "Do not be afraid." He speaks to us against anxiety and against our anxious attempts to be in control. He invites us to rest in his resurrection power. And the risen Lord stands in our midst and says, "Look at my hands and my feet." He points us beyond triumphalism toward the realization that the way of victory and triumph is in fact the way of the cross, the way of humbly serving others. May God grant us all a renewed and ever-renewing vision of the risen Lord who speaks against anxiety and calls beyond triumphalism.

Amen.

III. Eschatology and Nonviolent Witness: Yoder, Anabaptism, and Peace

"We've Read the End of the Book": An Engagement with Contemporary Christian Zionism through the Eschatology of John Howard Yoder (2008)

A Brief Introduction to American Christian Zionism[1]

Nearly two thousand people are gathered in a cavernous sanctuary. Pastor George takes the stage and welcomes the crowd. "We're here to say tonight that Jerusalem needs to remain—it must remain—the undivided capital under the control of Israel and the Jewish people." The crowd cheers. "It's not a political stance," adds Pastor George. "We're not political Zionists.

---

1. My knowledge of contemporary Christian Zionism arises from the following: (1) extensive analysis of the Scofield Reference Bible (1917); (2) contemporary Christian Zionist sources, including dozens of books, pamphlets, websites, and audio recordings; (3) one academic term spent with an American Christian Zionist congregation (referred to throughout as Pastor George's church), including observation of worship and all Israel-related classes, planning meetings, prayer meetings, and events, in addition to long, semi-structured interviews with all the pastors, staff, and core members of their pro-Israel ministry. Additionally, I visited and conducted interviews in the West Bank settlement which this congregation has "adopted." Historical background information is based on secondary sources, especially the following: Ariel, *On Behalf of Israel*; Boyer, *When Time Shall Be No More*; Kraus, *Dispensationalism in America*; Sandeen, *Roots of Fundamentalism*; Weber, *Living in the Shadow of the Second Coming*; and *On the Road to Armageddon*.

We're Bible Zionists." The lights go down for a forty-five minute multimedia production of music, dance, video, and narration telling the story of Jerusalem through the ages. The crowd stands and many sing along in Hebrew with a passionate rendition of *Hatikvah*, the Israeli national anthem. A local rabbi and a former Israeli ambassador give speeches. The peace process is ridiculed. An offering is collected. "Let's not forget, the city of Jerusalem needs to remain the undivided capital of the nation of Israel!" says Pastor George in closing. "Continue to pray for the peace of Jerusalem! Thank you for coming."

It is a Night to Honor Israel at an evangelical church in middle America. In the first year since the founding of Christians United for Israel (CUFI) by John Hagee in February of 2006, there were over fifty such gatherings across America, many of which have become annual events. Hagee's own church in Texas has been hosting an annual Night to Honor Israel since 1981, when Israel's bombing of Iraq's nuclear reactor moved him to "salute the Jewish people for what they'd done." Hagee is the most prominent leader of American Christian Zionism today, a movement with roots stretching back to the development of dispensational premillennialism in the nineteenth century.[2]

Dispensationalism is not only a particular form of premillennialist eschatology; it is a system of biblical hermeneutics, a philosophy of history, and a fairly comprehensive systematic theology. Formed by John Nelson Darby and the Plymouth Brethren in nineteenth-century Britain, dispensationalism took root in America around the turn of the century through the efforts of evangelicals who sponsored Bible conferences, established Bible institutes, and funded the development of the Scofield Reference Bible. C. I. Scofield's extensive notes and systems of chain references were first published by Oxford University Press in 1909 and became perhaps the most effective tool in the dissemination of dispensational doctrines. When the early twentieth century brought the consolidation of evangelicals from

2. I am speaking here only of the form of Christian Zionism which is currently most prominent in America. Historically, there have been many millenarianisms, hermeneutical strategies, and political ideologies which have motivated Christians to look forward to a Jewish homeland in Palestine. Further, though it is now commonly assumed that Christian Zionists are politically and theologically conservative, this was not the case before Israeli statehood. One of the most prominent Christian groups to support the creation of a Jewish state in the 1940s was the Christian Council on Palestine, the founding members of which included Reinhold Niebuhr and Paul Tillich.

diverse theological traditions into a more theologically cohesive fundamentalism, dispensationalism became one of its central features.[3]

Timothy Weber has likened the early dispensationalists to spectators
in a stadium, watching history unfold on the playing field below. There were
very few among them who believed they could or should play any role in
the fulfilment of prophecy except to be watchful and personally prepared.[4]
However, when Israel became a state in 1948 and expanded dramatically
in 1967, Weber argues that there was a profound shift. Dispensationalists
came down out of the stands and became active players on the field.[5] During the 1970s, Hal Lindsey's dispensationalist book *The Late Great Planet
Earth*[6] became an immensely popular best-seller. Dispensationalists began
forging new partnerships with American and Israeli Jews in support of
the state of Israel. Dispensationalists such as Jerry Falwell were central to
the rise of the new Christian right in the 1980s. Beginning in the 1990s,
dispensationalism was popularized for another generation in the ongoing
best-selling series of *Left Behind* novels. While popular novelists, televan-
gelists, and political activists were the public faces of dispensationalism,
there were also dozens of colleges and universities training thousands of
dispensationalist pastors, scholars, and lay people.

By the time John Hagee rose to prominence, there was an army of
Christians informed to varying degrees by dispensationalism, ready to be
mobilized. CUFI has become the primary mobilizing force of American
Christian Zionism, attracting thousands of delegates to their annual sum-
mits in Washington, DC, where they are addressed by American and Israeli
politicians such as Joseph Lieberman, John McCain, Dore Gold, and Benjamin Netanyahu. The delegates are given a briefing on the Middle East
and a set of talking points which they use in lobbying meetings with their
congressional representatives. At the 2007 summit, Hagee insisted that
CUFI's motives are entirely unrelated to eschatology. "Our support of Israel
has nothing to do with end-times prophecy," he said at the summit's press
conference. "It has absolutely nothing to do with eschatology." This claim is

3. On dispensationalism and fundamentalism, see Weber, *On the Road to Armageddon*; Marsden, *Fundamentalism and American Culture*.

4. Important exceptions included vocal proponents of Zionism, even prior to the rise
of the Jewish Zionist movement, such as William Blackstone, and the establishment of
many efforts to convert Jews to Christianity with the goal of sparing as many as possible
from the end-time tribulation.

5. Weber, *On the Road to Armageddon*.

6. Lindsey, *Late Great Planet Earth*.

difficult to reconcile with Hagee's own books, such as, *Beginning of the End: The Assassination of Yitzhak Rabin and the Coming Antichrist,* and *From Daniel to Doomsday: The Countdown Has Begun,* as well as the wider body of literature and rhetoric of Christian Zionists, much of which depends on dispensationalist end-times chronology.

Dispensationalism teaches that the world is locked in an inexorable downward spiral of ever-increasing incidence of immorality, apostasy, poverty, natural disaster, and war, and that these calamities will culminate in the rapid fulfilment of all end-times biblical prophecies over the course of seven years at the end of the present age.[7] First, the true church will be raptured, then the Beast will rule over the revived Roman empire and the Antichrist will be head of the remaining apostate church. Jews, having returned to the land of Israel "in unbelief"[8] will rebuild the temple, only to have it desecrated by the Beast when he turns on them, demanding to be worshiped. There will be a Great Tribulation, filled with every form of unprecedented human suffering. A remnant of 144,000 Jews will accept Jesus as Messiah and evangelize the troubled world, but two-thirds of them will be martyred, and the apostate church will be destroyed. Finally, the empire of the Beast will attack Israel in the battle of Armageddon, but Jesus will return in glory to destroy the Beast's forces, judge the Gentile nations for their treatment of Israel, be accepted as Messiah by all surviving Jews and Gentiles, and gather Jews into the land of Israel, where he will establish the kingdom, ruling the world from Jerusalem for one thousand years.

Most authors writing on Christian Zionism, both popular and scholarly, focus on this end-times cataclysm and argue or assume that Christian Zionists support Israel in order to hasten the advent of apocalypse, particularly the battle of Armageddon.[9] This can lead to imprecision

---

7. All quotations and citations from the Scofield Reference Bible are from the 1917 edition. Citations will refer to placement in relation to biblical texts instead of page numbers, as pagination may differ in various printings. The following end-times events are determined by a complex combination of prophetic texts, the book of Revelation, teachings of Jesus, and a few verses from the epistles. See Scofield's notes on the following texts: Isa 13:1; 13:9; 40:1; Jer 46:1; Ezek 20:37; 37:1; Dan 2:31; 7:8, 26; 8:9; Joel 1:4; 2:28; Micah 5:1, 7; Zech 13:8; 14:4; Mal 2:15; Matt 7:22; 24:3, 15, 16; 25:32; Luke 21:20; John 14:3; Acts 1:10–11; 1 Cor 15:52; 1 Thess 4:17; Rev 7:14; 13:1, 3, 6; 14:6; 16:19; 18:2; 19:17, 19, 20; 20:4, 10.

8. The descriptor "in unbelief" is a traditional dispensationalist phrase for Jews who have not accepted Jesus as Messiah.

9. In fact, it hardly seems possible to publish a book on Christian Zionism without including "Armageddon" in the title. See the following: Clark, *Allies for Armageddon;*

of—or complete lack of—engagement with the actual theology of American Christian Zionists, as well as simplistic conclusions about the danger of allowing politics to be informed by apocalyptic or eschatological convictions. In the following, I will use the thought of John Howard Yoder both as a device for serious engagement with dispensationalist Christian Zionism, and as a demonstration that responses to Christian Zionism by Christian ethicists require not the abandonment of apocalyptic and eschatology, but their well-articulated, alternative employment.[10]

Eschatology in John Howard Yoder

Those familiar with the importance of the historical Jesus and the church in Yoder's work may not be aware of the centrality of eschatology in his thought. However, centrality is not an overstatement.[11] Especially in *The Politics of Jesus* and *The Christian Witness to the State*, eschatology is at the core of Yoder's arguments. Yoder also wrote several essays which, at least in part, address the relationship between eschatology and ethics.[12] He insisted

Sizer, *Christian Zionism: Roadmap to Armageddon?*; Wagner, *Anxious for Armageddon*; Weber, *On the Road to Armageddon*; Wilson, *Armageddon Now!*

10. By focusing on eschatology, however, I am not claiming that end-times doctrines are *the* key to understanding and responding to Christian Zionists. Equally fruitful analyzes could focus on biblical hermeneutics, for example. Likewise, use of Yoder in the following analysis is not a claim that Yoder's eschatology is entirely sufficient theologically or as an antidote to dispensationalist eschatology. Various aspects of dispensationalism could be brought into relief through dialogue with a wide variety of theologians.

11. In one of the first single-author volumes written on Yoder, Craig Carter structures his argument around three themes: Christology as the source of Yoder's social ethics, eschatology as the context of Yoder's social ethics, and ecclesiology as the shape of Yoder's social ethics (Carter, *Politics of the Cross*). An entire volume has also been written on Yoder's eschatology: LeMasters, *Import of Eschatology in John Howard Yoder's Critique of Constantinianism*. Another author, arguing that Yoder can be characterized as a Pauline theologian, built his argument on two themes in Yoder: eschatology and justification (Harink, "Anabaptist and the Apostle").

12. Yoder, "Armaments and Eschatology"; "Ethics and Eschatology"; "Discerning the Kingdom of God in the Struggles of the World"; the following essays in *The Priestly Kingdom*: "Kingdom as Social Ethic," and "Constantinian Sources of Western Christian Ethics"; the following essays in *The Royal Priesthood*: "Otherness of the Church," "To Serve Our God and to Rule the World," "Peace without Eschatology?," "Christ, the Hope of the World"; "On Not Being in Charge," in Burns, *War and Its Discontents*; "Original Revolution," in *The Original Revolution*. Yoder also lectured at length on eschatology when he taught Mennonite seminary students. Some of these lectures are included in the collection, *Preface to Theology*.

that the apocalyptic texts of the Bible, too easily abandoned by moderns, are in fact relevant to shaping Christian eschatology. Though they were written within the conventions of the apocalyptic genre, they are actually more concerned with eschatology than apocalyptics.[13]

Yoder's Cross-Shaped Eschatology

According to Yoder, Jesus's ministry, death, and resurrection inaugurated a new aeon. In Luke's Gospel, Jesus proclaimed the arrival and described the character of the new aeon when he read from Isaiah in the synagogue in Nazareth.[14] The new aeon now coexists in tension with the old in the period between Pentecost and *parousia*. In fact, Yoder says, they may better be called "present" and "coming" aeons, rather than "old" and "new," because their distinction is not temporal; it is directional. The present aeon points backward to the human condition outside/before Christ; the coming aeon points forward to the full realization of the kingdom of God.[15]

Yoder believed that through the cross Jesus redefined kingship, politics, and power. Jesus did not reject the role of king, nor did he accept the prevailing Davidic interpretation of the coming king. Instead, he identified himself with Isaiah's suffering servant, thus redefining kingship.[16] Likewise, Jesus's kingdom is not non-political or apolitical; rather, Jesus redefined politics. He rejected the standard political options available to him: the revolutionary politics of the Zealots and the collaborating realism of the Sadducees, as well as the societal withdrawal of the Essenes and the religious ghetto of the Pharisees.[17] Yet he was gathering a political community with a political agenda. Thus, although the empire was mistaken in crucifying him as a revolutionary, they were not mistaken in identifying his message

13. Yoder defined eschatology as being concerned with "the meaning of the *eschaton* for present history," as differentiated from apocalyptics, which he defined as being concerned with specific information about the time and nature of the *eschaton* (Yoder, "Peace without Eschatology?," 145). While I am—and certainly Yoder was—aware of complex debates in other disciplines about the meanings of apocalyptic, apocalyptics, apocalypticism, etc., these cannot meaningfully be engaged here. I will simply allow Yoder's definitions to stand.

14. Yoder, *Politics of Jesus*, 31.

15. Yoder, *Christian Witness to the State*, 9; "Peace without Eschatology?," 146–49.

16. Yoder, *Preface to Theology*, 243–47. See also "To Serve Our God and to Rule the World," 133–34.

17. Yoder, "Original Revolution."

as political and subversive. Jesus, as king, is "the bearer of a new possibility of human, social, and therefore political relationships."[18] By inaugurating a new social order through willingly suffering to the point of death, Jesus also redefined power. The power of his kingdom is located precisely in the cross. "The cross is not a detour or a hurdle on the way to the kingdom, nor is it even the way to the kingdom; it is the kingdom come."[19]

The centrality of the cross for the character of Christ's reign is especially evident in Yoder's frequent use of Revelation 4–5, John's vision of four creatures, twenty-four elders, and myriad angels worshiping the Lamb who was slain, the only one in heaven or on earth worthy to open the scroll with seven seals. Yoder describes the scroll as containing the meaning of history, and it is *because* the Lamb was slain that he is worthy to open the scroll, worthy of honor, and worshiped by the multitudes. "[T]he cross and not the sword, suffering and not brute power determines the meaning of history."[20]

Yoder's Eschatologically Oriented Ecclesiology

Yoder emphasizes that the vision of worship in Revelation 4–5 is not only praise, it is "performative proclamation. It redefines the cosmos."[21] Part of the doxological redefinition of the cosmos[22] is that the Lamb gathers a priestly kingdom. Persons from every tribe and nation are gathered under the lordship of Christ to rule and reign with him.[23] Thus we find the church at the center of this revelation of the meaning of history. Yoder argues that the meaning of history is not worked out through violence or statecraft, but through worship, common life, and service to the world.[24]

However, the sovereignty of Christ is not exclusively manifested in the church. While the church is the present embodiment and anticipation

18. Yoder, *Politics of Jesus*, 52. See also *Christian Witness to the State*, 17.

19. Yoder, *Politics of Jesus*, 51.

20. Yoder, *Politics of Jesus*, 232. See also "Christ, the Hope of the World," 218.

21. Yoder, "Armaments and Eschatology," 53.

22. In one place, Yoder structures an entire presentation/essay around this theme. "To Serve Our God and to Rule the World" describes nine implications of seeing history doxologically.

23. Yoder, *Preface to Theology*, 248. See also "Peace without Eschatology?," 151.

24. See Yoder, *Christian Witness to the State*, 13; "Peace without Eschatology?," 151, 163; "Otherness of the Church," 56, 61.

of the ultimate triumph of God's redemption, and thus serves as the "scaf-folding" of history, the world, even in its rebellion, is ruled by Christ.[25] The church welcomes and honors societal progress in the world that is conso-nant with the coming kingdom, as measured by the criteria of the life and death of Jesus.[26] By "world," Yoder means the realm of human existence in which Christ's lordship is not recognized, as distinguished from the realm where there is willing submission to Christ; it is a distinction between hu-man responses. While Jesus's ethic is the ultimate standard for both realms, performance truly consonant with Jesus's *agape* is only possible in the realm where his lordship is recognized. This brings a kind of realism into Christian expectations of the capabilities of the state and what can be ac-complished in the world.[27]

Central to all aspects of Yoder's work is an argument about how the church has been corrupted by the Constantinian shift. Constantine is a sym-bol for Yoder; there is no simplistic suggestion that everything went wrong at the moment of Constantine's conversion. However, the legalization and later establishment of Christianity were decisive shifts in the church's his-tory. Yoder argues that one consequence was a reconceiving of eschatology. When the church was a powerless minority, Christians had to trust against visible evidence that God was governing history. What could be seen visibly was that there was a community of people worshiping and following Jesus. When the church became a broker and beneficiary of societal power, God's governance of history became a visible reality and the true church became invisible. Eschatology was realized; the millennial kingdom was identified with the empire.[28] According to Yoder, the Constantinian mistake allows

25. Yoder, *Christian Witness to the State*, 10–11.

26. Yoder, "Discerning the Kingdom of God in the Struggles of the World"; "To Serve Our God and to Rule the World," 132.

27. Yoder, *Christian Witness to the State*. On the issue of "realism," Nancey Murphy has noted that the difference between Yoder and Reinhold Niebuhr is not that Yoder was less realistic, but that they had two different eschatologies. Because Niebuhr begins with the question of whether the kingdom is temporal or eternal, he forces himself into a kingdom that transcends history so that "Christ's overcoming of the world can only mean that Christians know the meaning of history, not that history itself is transformed." In contrast, the kingdom is not wholly future or outside history in Yoder, since the two aeons coexist. See Murphy, "John Howard Yoder's Systematic Defense of Christian Paci-fism," 61–62. The most recent book on Yoder, while it does not feature eschatology as a major theme, makes a similar point about Yoder and Niebuhr with reference to eschatol-ogy: Nation, *John Howard Yoder*.

28. Yoder, "Constantinian Sources of Western Social Ethics," 136–38; "Otherness of

the church either to attempt to control society or to be content to serve as chaplain to those who think they control society. The eschatological corrective is that Christ governs history and the church only rules with Christ insofar as she rules as Jesus, through suffering service.

Yoder's Eschatologically Motivated and Restrained Social Ethics

It is my contention that Yoder's eschatology both motivates social action—a particularly important message for his own Mennonite tradition—and restrains social action—a particularly important response to the liberal social optimism of late-nineteenth and early twentieth-century theology. Eschatology as understood by Yoder does not propel Christians into the kind of optimistic "Christianizing" of society associated with the social gospel.[29] Nor does it make Christians helpless spectators of the world's suffering and injustice. Christian eschatology performs the twin functions of motivating social action and restraining it, of giving hope and insuring modesty.

One might be tempted to describe this dual function of eschatology through the well-worn categories of the "already" and the "not yet": because Christ has *already* won the victory, gathered the church, and sent the Holy Spirit, Christians are motivated and empowered to participate in God's redemptive purposes for all creation. Because Christ has *not yet* returned, finally subduing every power, and every knee does not yet bend to Christ's lordship, Christians are restrained from too much optimism and from acting as though we can make things turn out right. However, this description would miss what I believe is central to Yoder's particular interpretation of New Testament eschatology. It is precisely the nature of the *already* of Christ's reign that *both* motivates and restrains social action. *Because* Christ reigns, the church is reigning with him and her efforts to embody the earthly ministry of Christ are empowered and meaningful. And yet, Christ reigns *because* he chose suffering over violence and patience over

---

the Church," 57; "Peace without Eschatology?," 154–55. Yoder unfortunately attributes this shift to Augustine in ways that are not entirely fair. A more appropriate target for his critique would perhaps have been Eusebius. A more careful and sympathetic reading of Augustine's *City of God* reveals understandings of the city of God and the city of earth which are largely compatible with Yoder's understandings of the two realms—one in which Christ's sovereignty over all the earth is recognized though not yet fully realized, and another in which it is denied—as in *The Christian Witness to the State.*

29. For a comparison and contrast of Yoder's and Rauschenbusch's eschatologies, see Hütter, "Church."

coercion, so the church must also refuse attempts to seize power or control history. Thus God's eschatological word to the church, "Christ reigns," is a word both drawing her into social action and reminding her that she is not in control; instilling unshakable hope and restraining naive optimism; soliciting her participation and delimiting her means.

"Christ Reigns" as Invitation and Hope: Eschatology Motivates Social Action

For Yoder, faithful behavior is derived from the good news that Christ reigns, and obedience is made possible by the realities of the coming aeon in which the church already participates.[30] The coming kingdom makes human effort meaningful "because what God is going to do will be the fulfillment of human efforts, of human history."[31]

In the light of the *eschaton*, the church can discern what is right and wrong in the world and thereby offer valid critiques. For Yoder, revelation is about "how the crucified Jesus is a more adequate key to understanding what God is about in the real world of empires and armies and markets than is the ruler in Rome, with all his supporting military, commercial, and sacerdotal networks."[32] With this key, the church is able to offer both a valid critique of what is wrong,[33] as well as to "own the Lamb's victory in our own time,"[34] celebrating those things happening in the church and in the world that are consonant with the coming kingdom.

Not only a prophetic word of critique or celebration is made possible in light of the *eschaton*; the church also learns how to rule with Christ

30. See "To Serve Our God and to Rule the World," 136; *Preface to Theology*, 246; *Christian Witness to the State*, 9.

31. Yoder, *Preface to Theology*, 255.

32. Yoder, *Politics of Jesus*, 246. See also "To Serve Our God and to Rule the World," 132.

33. See "Peace without Eschatology?," 157.

34. Yoder, "To Serve Our God and to Rule the World," 137. In this passage Yoder speaks of the work of Martin Luther King Jr. as a specific example of the Lamb's victory in recent times. It should also be noted here that Yoder is not using eschatology as a programmatic key which will always ensure correct interpretation of events: "I do not claim that retrieving the apocalyptic idiom will be by itself a saving key to unlock otherwise lost truths. It is rather that . . . to reinstate the apocalyptic component of the Gospel may provide correctives at points where an immanentized hope in Christendom had robbed us of the capacity to discern bad news or to bring good" ("Armaments and Eschatology," 49).

through serving the world. She develops creative, nonviolent, "non-imperi-al strategies and tactics" for social action. Nonviolent, non-imperial action is only irrelevant, irresponsible, and/or ineffective if it is true that violence works and the meaning of history is in the hands of the rulers of empires. New Testament eschatology reveals, to the contrary, that nonviolence is the true power and that (as Yoder paraphrased Tolstoy) "progress in history is borne by the underdogs."[35] Therefore, although the faithful church renounces relevance, responsibility, and effectiveness as defined by the world, she finds that the nonviolent, servant way of Jesus is actually more relevant, responsible, and effective in the long run. "The church will be most effective where it abandons effectiveness and intelligence for the foolish weakness of the cross in which are the wisdom and the power of God."[36] For Yoder, such eschatologically shaped social action includes resistance efforts in the form of "militant non-cooperation,"[37] like the nonviolent resistance of the American civil rights movement. It also includes positive efforts to "pioneer" servant solutions to social ills, such as Anglo-Saxon democracy and the development of universities and hospitals, described by Yoder as pioneering efforts of the church which were then generalized for the benefit of entire societies.[38]

Christ-centered eschatology not only invites the church into social action, it provides a transcendent hope which sustains that action. Apocalyptic, Yoder suggests, calls into question standard accounts of moral reasoning which depend upon a closed cosmos of predictable causes and effects, and thereby opens the door to a non-consequentialist mode of moral reasoning: hope.[39] Christian hope and Christian ethics exist in a "spiral of complementarity, whereby the ethic supports the promise and vice versa, both of them contradicting both the fallen world's defeatism and the fallen

35. Yoder, "To Serve Our God and to Rule the World," 137.

36. Yoder, "Otherness of the Church," 64. See also "Christ, the Hope of the World," 215. For Yoder, this is not only a theory of what might be, but a verifiable description of what has been. "It can be argued that this is the lesson of history. The Christian church has been more successful in contributing to the development of society and to human well-being precisely when it has avoided alliances with the dominant political or cultural powers" ("Christ, the Hope of the World," 202).

37. Yoder, "Armaments and Eschatology," 56.

38. See Yoder, "Christ, the Hope of the World," 205; "To Serve Our God and to Rule the World," 135.

39. Yoder, "Ethics and Eschatology," 123.

Powers' oppression."[40] The "hope that our efforts seek to proclaim" is that Jesus is the Lord of history and God's Holy Spirit will make human efforts meaningful. Within this hope is the dimension of "wonder," that element of the unexpected which has characterized all the most important social movements.[41] The ethic sustained by eschatological hope is characterized by freedom—not only a *freedom from* needing to control, but precisely through the realization that the church cannot and need not control history comes the *freedom for* actively serving society.[42]

"Christ Reigns" as Limitation and Modesty: Eschatology Restrains Social Action

Let us first be very clear about what is meant here by restraint of social action. Contrary to many of Yoder's critics, Yoderian, eschatologically oriented ecclesiology does not trap Christians in an in-group sectarian church which has little or nothing to say or do in the world. In Yoder, eschatology restrains means of, optimism in, and conceptions of social action; it does not restrain the church from participating in social action in alliances with and for the benefit of the wider society.

Just as the reign of Christ is characterized by service and nonviolence, so is the presence of the church in the world. The *eschaton* is not an end which justifies all means; it is a revelation of the reality that it is the slaughtered Lamb who reigns and who calls us to be in the world as he is in the world. Rejecting violent and otherwise evil means is not a matter of purity or deontology; it is a matter of living in the reality that the cross and the church shaped by it are at the center of God's purposes in history.

Yoder's eschatology also prevents unrestrained optimism in the outcomes of social action. Because the two aeons exist in tension with one another, there will be no point in human history when the church can feel satisfied that her social efforts are complete. Additionally, these efforts will often have the short-term outcome of Jesus's own earthly efforts; namely, rejection and suffering. The eschatological hope of the church is very often a hope held against the evidence.

Jesus is the sovereign ruling Christ *because* he refused to take control of society and its history. "The universal testimony of Scripture is that

40. Yoder, "Ethics and Eschatology," 126.

41. Yoder, "Christ, the Hope of the World," 204–5.

42. See Yoder, *Politics of Jesus*, 187, 239–41.

Christians are those who follow Christ at just this point."[43] Thus the church cannot conceive of social action as effectiveness in leading society toward its proper goal or pushing society toward peace and justice. Christian social action must be conceived of as faithfulness to Christ through service and witness. "Since we are not the lord of history there will be times when the only thing we can do is to speak and the only word we can speak is the word clothed in a deed, a word that can command attention from no one and that can coerce no one."[44]

Yoder on Apocalyptic and the People of God

When Yoder was assigned the topic "armaments and eschatology" for the 1987 gathering of the Society for the Study of Christian Ethics, he made a presentation on the use of apocalyptic discourse in the arms race. He demonstrated the apocalyptic dimension of the arms race debate, "the claim that we have entered a brand new age, where the old continuities and criteria no longer count,"[45] and the dynamic of the nuclear threat being considered so dire as to legitimate ethical discourse "off the scale of the more careful forms" otherwise practiced.[46] While Yoder was critical of such claims, his contention was that their illegitimacy was not due to the illegitimacy of apocalyptic discourse *per se*. In fact, Yoder criticized then-recent biblical scholarship and its use by theologians which suggested that seemingly foreign and difficult apocalyptic materials (defined here as texts treating the end of history) should be disregarded in favor of more easily generalized and applied eschatology (defined here as the treatment of God's action in human history). Yoder contended that the setting aside of apocalyptic in favor of an "immanentized hope in Christendom has robbed us of the capacity to discern bad news or to bring good," and that a recovery of valid forms and uses of apocalyptic was needed.[47] Such a retrieval, Yoder suggested, may necessitate criteria for the purpose of distinguishing between valid and less valid forms of apocalyptic: "What might it then be about the

43. Yoder, *Politics of Jesus*, 234.
44. Yoder, "Christ, the Hope of the World," 204.
45. Yoder, "Armaments and Eschatology," 45.
46. Yoder, "Armaments and Eschatology," 47.
47. Yoder, "Armaments and Eschatology," 49.

visions of history which made sense for the early witnesses, which we might with proper care appropriate?"[48]

Yoder went on to describe how apocalyptic "deconstructs" four facets of the way things seem to be: Caesar seems to be the one moving history, Christian moral rules seem to need adjustment to suit the profession of Caesar, cause-and-effect/lesser-of-two-evils judgments seem reliable, and Christian ethics seems readily and unproblematically translatable into morality for everyone. Yoder implied that these were his criteria for valid apocalyptic; valid apocalyptic deconstructs these four assumptions. However, the list of four assumptions clearly functions more to continue his argument against Constantinianism than as constructive work on apocalyptic. Except, that is, for the few brief paragraphs in which Yoder describes what he means by deconstruction. In this description of deconstruction we find a threefold movement of apocalyptic in the believing community. I suggest that it is in these three movements, rather than in the list of four assumptions Yoder offered, that we find the criteria needed for assessing forms of apocalyptic:

1. *Deconstruction: Things are not as they seem.* Yoder cited ethicist Larry Rasmussen who has suggested that apocalyptic is a vehicle for the believing community to "'deconstruct' the self-evident picture of how things are which those in power use to explain that they cannot but stay that way."[49] Valid use of apocalyptic does not affirm the status quo; rather, it questions standard accounts and opens the possibility of seeing reality differently. The reader or audience of authentic apocalyptic discourse becomes aware that social and political realities are not as they seem.

2. *Proclamation: Oppressive power is not the final word.* Yoder built on Rasmussen's point with his own: the sorts of suffering minority communities from which biblical apocalyptic arose need "first of all to know not what they would do if they were rulers, nor how to seize power, but that the present power constellation which oppresses them is not the last word."[50] Apocalyptic is a vehicle through which the people of God receive and make the proclamation of the reality that

48. Yoder, "Armaments and Eschatology," 51.
49. Yoder, "Armaments and Eschatology," 53.
50. Yoder, "Armaments and Eschatology," 53.

God is in control, not those who seek to control others through oppression and violence.

3. *Empowerment: Speaking truth to power.* Yoder then visited, as he nearly always had in writings on eschatology, the first vision of John in Revelation, calling the hymnody reflected there "performative proclamation" which "redefines the cosmos in a way prerequisite to the moral independence which it takes to speak truth to power."[51] Valid apocalyptic proclaims a different reality which is not only for the sake of encouraging beleaguered believers, but is extended through empowerment of the people of God to speak truth to oppressive power.

THE CROSS IN DISPENSATIONALIST ESCHATOLOGY

The central features of Yoder's eschatology—its cruciform character which in turn orients ecclesiology and both motivates and restrains social action—as demonstrated above are well suited to the task of engaging the theology and ethics of contemporary American Christian Zionism which have been shaped by the dispensational system which Darby developed and the Scofield Reference Bible popularized.

A key concept in Scofield is the sharp distinction between the two advents of Jesus Christ. According to Scofield, prophecies concerning a suffering, rejected servant foretold the first advent. Prophecies of a victorious, conquering king foretell the second advent. The prophets themselves were not aware that there would be two advents, so they were confused by their blended visions of suffering and victory.[52] According to Scofield, the problem of what seemed like contradictory visions to the prophets was "solved by partial fulfillment."[53] That is, only the rejection and suffering aspects were fulfilled in Christ's first advent; the aspects of glory and power will not be fulfilled until he returns.[54] In dispensationalism, Jesus came as a king and offered the nation of Israel the opportunity to accept the kingdom he described in his teachings, but the nation officially rejected him in the

---

51. Yoder, "Armaments and Eschatology," 53.

52. According to Scofield, 1 Pet 1:10–11 describes the prophets' limited vision in this regard.

53. See Scofield's note on Acts 1:11.

54. See also Scofield's notes on Matt 13:17 and Mal 3:1, as well as Scofield's introduction to the prophetic books, "The Prophetical Books," immediately preceding Isaiah.

crucifixion.[55] The cross stands as a tragic symbol of failure. Victory is found in the cross only through substitutionary atonement.

Whereas for Yoder, the cross is the inauguration of the aeon of the coming kingdom—and in the cross Jesus redefines kingship, politics, and power—in dispensationalism, the cross signals the postponement of the intended kingdom, which will only be made manifest when Jesus returns as the Davidic king, exercising precisely the form of political power Yoder claims Jesus rejected. For Yoder, Jesus is worshiped and glorified because he was slain, and it is in his suffering to the point of death that we find the meaning of human history. In dispensationalism, we will not see Jesus in his glory until he returns as a conquering warrior and theocratic ruler. Ultimate meaning is located in the future fulfilment of promises to the nation of Israel. In Yoder, the *eschaton* reveals the positive centrality of the cross, while in dispensationalism the *eschaton* corrects the tragedy of the cross.

While many Christian Zionists today are no longer so steeped or invested in the entire dispensationalist system, the doctrine of the two advents has a continuing legacy in their popular Christology. Jesus is spoken of virtually exclusively in terms of either atonement or second coming. The following is an excerpt from the most widely read and recommended book among the Christian Zionists at Pastor George's church:

> What the rabbis were not able to understand was that the portraits of the Messiah would be fulfilled in one person, but not at the same time. There would be a time gap between the two roles the Messiah would play. This would require him to appear on planet earth at two different times. The first time He would come as the religious Messiah to bring atonement for sin and establish the spiritual realm of the kingdom of God in the hearts of men. Then after a period of time, he would come again as the political-military Messiah to establish the physical kingdom of God over all the earth and the physical kingdom of David to administer it along with the resurrected believers of all ages.[56]

When members of the congregation were asked about the importance of Jesus having come to earth, their answers were almost exclusively related to atonement understood in terms of substitution and satisfaction. When discussing the teachings of Jesus, the text they most often highlighted was the Olivet Discourse, the two chapters of Matthew which they take

55. See Scofield's notes on Matthew 4:17 and 21:4.

56. Booker, *Blow the Trumpet in Zion*, 171.

as Jesus's own literal description of the Great Tribulation and his second coming (Matthew 24–25). The legacy of dispensationalism in their Christology is a deeply divided soteriology which sees the individual soul saved through the first advent but embodiment and sociality unredeemable until the second advent.

Ecclesiology and Dispensationalist Eschatology

According to Scofield, because it was not revealed to or through the prophets that there would be two separate advents, there were no prophecies about the intervening period of time. God's ultimate plan for humanity—theocratic rule centered in Jerusalem—has to do with Israel, not the church. The church is neither the new Israel nor the fulfilled kingdom.[57] Prophetic chronology provided specific dates for events between the prophets and the coming of Messiah, and for events surrounding Messiah's second coming, but the gap between the two comings was unknown to the prophets and therefore impossible to chart chronologically.[58] The rejection of Jesus at his first advent opened a rift in prophetic time, during which the church came into existence. When the dispensation of the church has run its course, the true church will be raptured from the earth and the prophetic clock will once again begin to tick.

The nature of the dispensations, for which this form of theology is named, is that in each age God deals with humanity through particular means, and humanity is tested in regard to those means. Humanity inevitably fails the test, God executes judgment, and a new dispensation begins. Failure and judgment have already occurred in relation to the dispensations

57. See Scofield's introduction to the Gospels, "The Four Gospels," immediately preceding Matthew.

58. Much of dispensationalism hinges on this interpretation, particularly of Daniel 9. The "seventy weeks" are interpreted as "sevens of years; seventy weeks of seven years each," or a total of 490 years. Sixty-nine of the seventy weeks (483 years) have already been fulfilled. In seven weeks (forty-nine years), the temple was rebuilt, as recorded in Ezra and Nehemiah. After sixty-two weeks (434 years), Messiah arrived in the birth of Jesus of Nazareth, and after that he was "cut off" by his rejection and crucifixion. The one week (seven years) of verse 27 remains to be fulfilled, and between the fulfilled 483 years and the unfulfilled seven years stands the indeterminate "unto the end" of verse 26, which is the present age. In the final week (seven years), all the remaining prophecies preceding the kingdom age will be fulfilled. The events described in verse 27 as occurring "in the midst of the week," are aspects of the Great Tribulation. See Scofield's notes on Daniel 9, particularly 9:24.

of innocence, conscience, human government, promise, and law.[59] The present dispensation of grace, or the church age, is destined to end likewise. While there will continue to be faithful individuals, their unity with one another, like their unity with Christ, is mysterious and invisible. The visible church is becoming increasingly apostate, and will continue its decline until Jesus catches up the true, invisible church in the rapture and abandons the visible church to ruin under the headship of the Antichrist.[60] According to Scofield, when Jesus was rejected and crucified, God turned away from Israel as the focus of divine action and intention. When the true church is raptured and the visible church falls, Jesus will return and be recognized by Israel as Messiah; God will turn away from the church and resume the ultimate plan for humanity through a worldwide theocracy, ruled by Jesus from Jerusalem.[61]

For both Yoder and dispensationalists, the meaning of human history is revealed eschatologically. However, while this results in an eschatologically oriented ecclesiology in Yoder, it results in an eschatologically attenuated ecclesiology in dispensationalism. Yoder's reading of revelation finds ultimacy in the worshiping community gathered around the Lamb that was slain. Scofield's reading locates ultimacy in Christ's violent destruction of the nations and establishment of the kingdom on earth. In the meantime, Yoder sees a crucial distinction between faithful and unfaithful responses to Christ's lordship, and faithfulness must be embodied in visible communal life. Contrary to post-Constantinian eschatologies, God's sovereign reign over all the earth is currently hidden, but the true church should be visible. In dispensationalism, the crucial distinction is between the church and Israel, and in this regard, what went wrong in the Constantinian era was the development of supersessionism, identification of the church as the new Israel. In dispensationalist Christian Zionism, the true church is

59. The dispensations are not purely linear and consecutive. Different dispensations apply to different people groups differently. The dispensation of human government ended for Israel in the judgment of captivities, but will not end for Gentiles until Jesus returns to judge the nations. The dispensations of promise and law applied only to Israel. Scofield's notes on the dispensations begin at Gen 1:28, and can be traced from there through his chain of references.

60. On the true invisible church, see Scofield's notes on Matt 13:45 and Heb 12:23. On the visible church and apostasy see notes on 1 Tim 3:15; 2 Tim 3:1; Rev 1:20; and his introduction to Ephesians, "The Epistle of Paul the Apostle to the Ephesians."

61. See Scofield's notes on Matt 21:43 and Rom 11:1.

invisible, but God's sovereign reign is readily observable in the existence of the modern state of Israel.

The specifics of dispensationalist ecclesiology are unknown to many rank and file Christian Zionists. When dispensationalism first arrived in America, nineteenth-century evangelicals were captivated by Darby's eschatology but uneasy with the pessimistic ecclesiology which grew from his own break with the Anglican Church. They did not abandon their congregations and denominations in favor of Plymouth Brethren-esque meetings, as Darby urged.[62] However, the seeds of Darby's stop-gap, apostate church bear fruit today in the extremely thin ecclesiology of many evangelical Christian Zionists. For them, the church's main functions are to save individual souls, to encourage and strengthen the individual, and to encourage and strengthen the state of Israel.

When asked what should be the top priorities of the church, Pastor George said salvation, believing Jesus Christ is the Messiah, and supporting Israel. Then he seemed at a loss to name anything else. He said, "Then, I mean, along with those, well, I don't think anything else, you know, you'd have to give me an example of what would even be [a] higher [priority] than that." Other members of the congregation spoke of the purpose of the church mainly in terms of evangelism and preventing one another from weakening in or falling away from faith. The central role of the church in relation to society is support of Israel. Individual salvation is the purview of the church, and during the church age, Christ reigns in individual hearts. Societal transformation will be the purview of Israel and the socio-political reign of her Messiah.

Dispensationalist Eschatology as Motivation and Restraint of Social Ethics

The role of dispensationalism in the social ethics of fundamentalism and evangelicalism is a long-debated issue among American church historians. Some have suggested that dispensationalist eschatology single-handedly transformed the socially progressive and activist evangelicals of the nineteenth century into the inwardly focused and socially conservative fundamentalists of the twentieth century.[63] Others have insisted that the

---

62. See Kraus, *Dispensationalism*, 55–56; Ariel, *On Behalf of Israel*, 25; Sandeen, *Roots of Fundamentalism*, 79.

63. Timothy Smith called this "the great reversal," and his thesis was carried forward

transformation was neither that stark nor attributable to that one factor.[64] While the latter, more nuanced argument has become something of a consensus, it is nonetheless agreed that the fatalism inherent in dispensationalism has contributed to fundamentalist social inertia.

How and why the fundamentalists of the early twentieth century became the evangelicals who were so successfully politically mobilized in the mid- to late-twentieth century is an ongoing matter of research and discussion among historians, sociologists, and scholars specializing in the American religious right. What is clear is that many thousands—perhaps millions—of evangelical Christians are currently deeply motivated to act on behalf of the interests of the state of Israel, as they perceive them. Their Zionist social action takes a wide variety of forms, from humanitarian assistance for poor Israeli immigrants, to lobbying the United States government to refrain from restraining Israel's military; from recruiting poor Russians to become Israeli settlers, to praying for the elimination of Israel's enemies.

Pastor George's congregation engages in social action in support of Israel through seeking to educate Christians about Israel and raise awareness among Jews about Christian Zionism; through political lobbying which focuses primarily on Israel's military being free from international restraint; through financial support of several pro-Israel organizations, both Christian and Jewish; and through spending their tourism dollars in Israel. The congregation also sends a performance group of teens and twenty-somethings to Israel every summer to do a tour of military bases where they seek to demonstrate through entertaining song and dance that God loves the Jewish people and blesses the Israeli military in defending their promised land. And the congregation has "adopted" an Israeli settlement in the West Bank, making significant contributions of money, resources, and time to support the settlement, improve the quality of life there, and encourage the beleaguered settlers.

In Yoder's eschatology, Christology and ecclesiology meet in both motivation and restraint of social action. The lamb that was slain reigns in heaven and earth, gathering and empowering a worshiping community to act meaningfully in human history through non-consequentialist, non-violent, non-imperial social action. Among the Christian Zionist heirs of

by Martin Marty and Timothy Weber. See Smith, *Revivalism and Social Reform*; Marty, *Righteous Empire*; Weber, *Living in the Shadow of the Second Coming*.

64. See especially Marsden, *Fundamentalism and American Culture*.

dispensationalism, Christ's social relevance is relegated to the end of days, violent establishment of a global, theocratic empire, and the primary social relevance of the church lies in cooperation with God's setting of the stage for this end-time drama. Social action motivated by this eschatology includes virtually anything which serves to bring more Jews to Israel, strengthen Israel's military, and broaden and sustain Israel's claims to land. For Christian Zionists, questions about consequentialism are irrelevant because of the utter certainty of future events. Questions about violence and militarism are irrelevant because the Bible clearly teaches that God has used and will use violence—both human and divine—in the shaping of Israel's destiny. Questions about imperialism are irrelevant as history is destined to culminate in world-wide theocratic empire. "We've read the end of the book," goes a common saying among Christian Zionists. "And guess what? We win!"

A more lengthy project of this sort could fruitfully proceed to employ the criteria developed from Yoder above for the analysis of dispensationalist apocalypticism. However, such an analysis would require far more extensive description of Christian Zionist belief and practice than is possible here. What has been established is that when simplistic stereotype and sensationalist exposé are abandoned in favor of serious critical engagement with contemporary Christian Zionism, opportunities arise for deeper understanding and more constructive response. Beyond the caricatures of wild fundamentalists ushering in the apocalypse, we find a complex system of convictions and practices in which eschatology subordinates ecclesiology and Christology, severing social ethics from the Christological and ecclesiological sources required for properly Christian theological ethics. The use of Yoder's work to bring this system into relief further establishes that eschatology *per se* is not inimical to the formation of Christian social ethics, which can and should be positively formed by the eschatological revelation of the reality and nature of Christ's reign. It is the misshapen eschatology resulting from complex hermeneutical moves intended to sustain strict biblicism and biblical literalism which nurtures the Christian Zionist social ethics which have become so problematic in our time.

CHAPTER 9

Doctrines of "The Two": The Church and the Elusive "Public" in Augustine and Yoder (2017)

In his introduction to political theology, Michael Kirwan begins his historical overview under the heading "the doctrine of the Two," a phrase he draws from a letter of Pope Gelasius to Emperor Anastasius: "Two there are, august Emperor, by which this world is ruled: the consecrated authority of priests and the royal power."[1] Along with Kirwan, we can observe that at least as early as Augustine, Christian political theology has revolved around doctrines, or at least questions, of "the two." Augustine's two cities, medieval theories of two swords, the crises of two authorities surrounding investiture and conciliarism, Luther's two kingdoms, and modern debates of church and state. In one sense, these are different iterations of the same question: the relationship of the authorities, institutions, and claims intrinsic to Christianity to the authorities, institutions, and claims of governments and societies. However, in another sense, each instance is dealing with a different set of two entities: the two cities, swords, authorities, kingdoms, etc., have not been synonymous with or collapsible into one another. They have variously addressed two citizenships, two sovereignties, two spheres of life, and two institutions.

In contemporary political theology, one of the most pervasive iterations of "the two" seems to be "church" and "public." Ordinands are taught

1. Kirwan, *Political Theology,* ch. 4.

how to do "public theology." Denominations have separate offices and committees for church issues and public issues. We participate in endless debates about the role of the church in the public square. Christians in academia, ministry, and politics constantly refer to the church and the public as if we all know what we are talking about. But one need only to scratch the surface to see that the "public" is an elusive entity or realm, defying clear definition, especially in binary relation to "church." As William Cavanaugh has incisively argued in his work on so-called religious violence, when scholars say "we all know what we mean" when we use a word like "religion," there is very good reason to believe that something is wrong.[2] And I believe something is wrong with our continuing assumption that we all know what we mean when we say "public."

I have argued,[3] along with others (most notably, Daniel Bell[4] and James Smith[5]), that one of the clear distinctions between the schools of political theology which first emerged in the mid-twentieth century (including European political theology, various forms of liberation, Black, and feminist theologies, and Anglo-American public theologies) and the next generation of political theology which emerged in the late-twentieth century (including postliberalism, Radical Orthodoxy, and some forms of so-called contextual theologies) has been a shift away from binary views of "church" and "public," in which the task is either translation from the particularism of the church into the universalism of the public or correlation between what was received through revelation in the church and what has arisen through secular reasoning in public.

For many, the death knell was sounded for translationist and correlationist approaches with Hauerwas's "Let the church be the church,"[6] and Milbank's "Once, there was no secular."[7] Hauerwas insisted that the task of Christian social ethics was not to translate Christian convictions and practices into public applications, rather more fully to embody those convictions and practices *as the church.* Thus his well know dictum, "The church does not have a social ethic; the church is a social ethic."[8] Milbank insisted

---

2. Cavanaugh, *Myth of Religious Violence*, 16.

3. Phillips, *Political Theology*, 50–51.

4. Bell, "State and Civil Society," 423–38.

5. Smith, *Introducing Radical Orthodoxy*, 41–42.

6. This phrase and concept echoes throughout Hauerwas's corpus.

7. Milbank, *Theology and Social Theory*, 9.

8. Hauerwas, *Peaceable Kingdom*, 99.

that the notion of the "secular" as a separate realm of human life upon which claims of transcendence have no bearing was a fictitious construct of the modern era. Following either line of reasoning, the legitimacy of framing political theology either in terms of translating particularly Christian convictions and practices into secular, public applications, or of correlating Christian insights with secular, public wisdom, became indefensible. The church as properly public and the secular public as theological and even sectarian have become bywords of large segments of contemporary Christian theology.

Yet our use of the word "public" seems undiminished. This is not surprising, of course, among those who have not identified with postliberalism or Radical Orthodoxy; "public theology" is alive and well. However, it is not only within the ranks of public theologians that the term "public" continues to hold sway. Others who may not identify with the "public theology" approach find continuing relevance in the term, such as in Charles Mathewes's *A Theology of Public Life*, Gavin D'Costa's *Theology in the Public Square*, and Jennifer McBride's *The Church for the World: A Theology of Public Witness*. Even theologians more explicitly sympathetic to postliberalism and Radical Orthodoxy continue to use these phrases, as seen in Rowan Williams's *Faith in the Public Square*.

Many scholars have sought to clarify what "secular" does and does not mean, and whether or how we should use such a word. Some argue that no such thing as "secularism" ever really happened (it was a thesis which has been disproven), and that the "secular sphere" is a pure fiction. Others believe there is an important, continued use for a certain form of the word, carefully distinguished from other uses. Rowan Williams has in many places distinguished "procedural secularism" from "programmatic secularism": the procedural variety can open up possibilities for multiple religious groups as it is a lack of enforcement or preference for one particular faith tradition, but the programmatic variety seeks to free common life from religion and to banish faith to the realm of private belief. A different but related distinction has been made by Eric Gregory, who defends "secularity" over-against "secularism," where secularism is the advocacy of a sphere which is free from religion, transcendence, metaphysics, and matters of personal value and morality; while secularity is "a shared time afforded all humanity by the common grace of God" which "opens the door for a separation of the political and the ecclesial without separating morality from politics or condemning the religious to private subjectivity."[9] While there have been many discussions of the concept of the "public square," analyses of the word "public" itself—analogous to those of "secular" in Williams, Gregory, and many others—are surprisingly absent.

Let me be clear: I have no objection *per se* to the word "public." It will very obviously continue to be useful in many contexts. My problem is that I cannot imagine a definition of "public" in relation to the common life of peoples, societies, and states in which the churches are something other than "public." It is specifically how our unexamined use of "public" allows us to continue to frame it in binary relation to "church" which concerns me, not the word "public" itself. If, then, the church/public binary is not the best way of framing the question of "the two" in contemporary contexts, what is? I will argue for a "doctrine of the two" which attends to both the early origins of Christian political thought and to more recent shifts in political theology by using as its key interlocutors Augustine of Hippo and John Howard Yoder.

Even if such a thing were historically possible, these two men, on their own terms, and in my opinion due to each of their own worst instincts, would themselves have had no interest in speaking to one another. We can be relatively certain that Augustine would have no patience with Yoder's Anabaptist tradition (and that the later Augustine would likely even support the violent suppression of such a movement). And we know without question that Yoder had no patience for Augustine. Yoder resented Augustine both as architect of the just war tradition and as a key influence for Reinhold Niebuhr. He blamed Augustine for enshrining in orthodoxy the Constantinian shift from the visibility to the invisibility of the true church,[10] and he erroneously accused him of equating the Roman Church with the kingdom of God: "It is not at all surprising that Augustine, for whom the Constantinian church was a matter of course, should have held that the Roman church was the millennium. Thus the next step in the union of church and world was the conscious abandon of eschatology."[11] Even setting anachronism aside, there is little reason to hope either of these men could have had any desire to see connections between their theologies.

However, I am not the first theologian to put Augustine and Yoder in conversation with one another. In a Duke University doctorate, Charles

9. Gregory, *Politics and the Order of Love*, 78.
10. Yoder, "Otherness of the Church," 57–58.
11. Yoder, "Peace without Eschatology?," 154.

Collier pursues the possibility of a nonviolent Augustinianism.[12] The most explicit example I know of which has been widely published is Gerald Schlabach's essay, "The Christian Witness in the Earthly City: John Howard Yoder as Augustinian Interlocutor."[13]

In this piece, which has been published in multiple volumes on Yoder's work, Schlabach briefly listed six ways in which Augustine's *City of God* and Yoder's *The Christian Witness to the State* corresponded with one another:[14] (1) their frame of reference was eschatological; (2) they both described two societies which are presently intermixed yet distinguishable by their differing ends and loves; (3) both maintained that "the purpose of history and the good of the social order are never knowable on their own terms";[15] (4) both "made thorough-going critiques of imperial presumption";[16] (5) both described government as limited in its capacity to effect peace and justice, and both expected Christians to keep calling their governments to do better; and finally, (6) both described the Christian's motivation for seeking the peace of the earthly city in terms of how the earthly city could aid the mission of the church, which is the true purpose of history.

Schlabach drew these parallels in order to argue "that an Augustinian can be a pacifist and a pacifist an Augustinian," an argument with which I whole-heartedly agree, but which is not my purpose to pursue here. Instead, I want to expand upon Schlabach's noted commonalities between Augustine's two cities and Yoder's two orders, to propose a constructive way of imagining "the two" which is not troubled by the binary of the church and the elusive "public."

In stark contrast to Augustine's magisterial *De Civitate Dei*, Yoder's *The Christian Witness to the State* can hardly even be called a book. It was originally a pamphlet which Yoder produced for the Institute of Mennonite Studies in the late 1950s. It is brief, it contains hand-drawn illustrations which now seem almost comical, and it is rife with dated conventions, especially gender-exclusive language about "the statesman." Although Yoder's use of gender in language improved dramatically during his career, no treatment of Yoder today can ignore the recent revelations of the

---

12. Collier, "Nonviolent Augustinianism?"

13. Schlabach, "Christian Witness in the Earthly City"; and Dula and Huebner, *New Yoder*, 18–41.

14. Schlabach, "Christian Witness in the Earthly City," 231–33.

15. Schlabach, "Christian Witness in the Earthly City," 232.

16. Schlabach, "Christian Witness in the Earthly City," 232.

undeniable extent to which he abused and manipulated women throughout most of his adult life.[17]

However, for all its and his shortcomings, Yoder's *The Christian Witness to the State* proposed a compelling answer to "the question of the two." Yoder was both a devout Anabaptist from a long Mennonite tradition and a dedicated ecumenist. The central argument of *Christian Witness* arose from Yoder's life-long dual quest: to convince his fellow Mennonites to be less sectarian, and to convince his fellow ecumenists that Anabaptism had truly catholic relevance.

Thus, he made his proposal over-against the traditional Anabaptist view that governments exist "outside the perfection of Christ," and that Christians, in order to live in the perfection of Christ, must remain separate from these institutions which operate with a different ethical horizon. He likewise argued over and against the view of non-pacifist Christians that pacifist Christianity, guided by the love ethic of Jesus's teachings, must necessarily be irrelevant to and therefore silent in all matters of the realm of society and government, a realm guided by the ethic of justice which often requires acts and institutions of coercion and violence. The pamphlet was both a pastoral exhortation to his own community and an apology to those criticizing his community's tradition.

This is not without analogy to Augustine's twin purposes in the face of the declining Roman empire: to convince his own community that they had not conceived of their relationship to temporal powers correctly (having too closely wed the success of the gospel and the coming of the kingdom with the power of the Roman empire), and to convince those outside his own community of the relevance of his faith (as an apology to pagan Romans who were blaming Christianity for Rome's failure). Augustine argued that no human empire is ultimate: the empire cannot establish true peace or true justice; it is God's work of salvation which is the meaning of history, not the workings of emperors. Yoder argued that the meaning of history is borne in the church, not in statecraft, because "the church points forward

---

17. The full extent of Yoder's consistent pattern of abuse came into public view especially with Oppenheimer, "Theologian's Influence, and Stained Past, Live On." Since then, an extensive process has been pursued by Mennonites in America, especially at Anabaptist Mennonite Biblical Seminary where Yoder taught before spending the remainder of his career at Notre Dame University, which has involved listening to Yoder's victims and coming to terms with how his destructive behavior was allowed to continue. See also the special issue of *Mennonite Quarterly Review* 89 (January 1, 2015) dedicated to the topic of Yoder's sexual abuse.

as the social manifestation of the ultimately triumphant redemptive work of God."[18]

According to Yoder, there are two orders, both of which are ruled over by Christ, which are distinguished from one another by their responses to Christ's rule. The order of providence is where Christ reigns over the response of disobedience through the powers. The order of redemption is where Christ reigns through the obedience of his disciples. Yoder also describes these as two realms, one in which faith in Christ is presupposed, and one in which faith is not a presupposition. The analogies with Augustine are clear: the two cities are distinguished from one another by their differing loves and orientations, the heavenly city pointing toward the love and worship of God, and the earthly city pointing toward love and fulfillment of self instead of worship of God.

Most important for our purposes here: both formulations of "the two" conceive of the two realities in question as complex spatio-temporal realities. Most conceptions of "the two" remove the temporal element, and give varying answers to the question of how current social space should be divided into distinct spheres, whether these are spheres of the institutions of church and government or spheres of spiritual and secular authority, or spheres of private associations and public engagement. But Augustine, as William Cavanaugh has noted, "does not map the two cities out in space, but rather projects them across time," and in this sense the two cities have more to do with the already and the not yet than with sacred and secular or private and public.[19] So too with Yoder's two orders, one in which Christ's lordship is already, though imperfectly, recognized and embodied in time and space, and the other in which Christ's lordship is just as real but is not yet recognized.

In both Augustine and Yoder, one of "the two" is identified with but not absolutely equated with the church. Although Augustine occasionally refers to the city of God as the church, the entirety of his descriptions makes it clear that the city's citizens are all those who worship God, in heaven and on earth, throughout all history and into eternity. The church is that part of the city of God which currently sojourns on earth. So too, Yoder identifies the church with the order of redemption in which faith in Christ is presupposed. Yet, by clarifying that this realm is not the church as such, and that the order of providence where faith in Christ is not a presupposition is not

18. Yoder, *Christian Witness to the State*, 10.

19. Cavanaugh, "From One City to Two," 59.

the state as such, he similarly broadens and complexifies his notion of "the two." For both theologians, this city or order which is identified with the church is also a reality which is bigger than any specific instantiation in the churches. And while both Augustine and Yoder are very concrete and specific about what characterizes the citizens of this city, in both cases it is impossible in the current age of coexisting aeons to point to any individual and say this person is in or out; both theologians acknowledge that human responses to God are more complicated than that.

What, then, is the role of the church in relation to the second of "the two": the earthly city in Augustine and the order of providence in Yoder? The key theme for Augustine is sojourning: the church is that part of the city of God which exists as a pilgrim people alongside the earthly city during the present age. While on pilgrimage here and now, the church makes use of all the same goods as the earthly city, but with a different orientation and aim. The church employs the conventions, institutions, laws, and practices of the present time and place—all the goods with which the earthly city can only manage to establish some faint shadows of justice and peace—alongside her own distinctive institutions and practices, all for the love and worship of God, as participants in the eternal justice and peace which only God can establish and which can only exist in that city which is devoted to God.

The key theme for Yoder is witness. The church knows the ultimate reality for which all things are created and to which all things are called, and so she bears witness to that reality through her own life within the order of redemption, and by calling the people and institutions of the order of providence ever closer to their created purposes. This is the meaning of evangelism. The *agape* ethic of Jesus is at the heart of the church's witness, as she seeks to embody that ethic in her life within the order of redemption and as she seeks to help the order of providence as it currently exists to come closer to that ethical horizon.

Thus, in both Augustine and Yoder we find a "doctrine of the two" in which there is no thoroughgoing dualism of sacred versus secular, public versus private, church versus world, or church versus state. It is a "doctrine of the two" in which there is no flat map of space which is carved into two spheres of influence or authority. Instead there is a complex, multidimensional mapping in space and across time of differing responses and orientations of humans toward God. And while the heavenly city and the order of redemption cannot be limited to or equated with the church, these "doctrines of the two" still have much to say about how the church is meant to live in the world. I see at least five important similarities between Augustine's and Yoder's understandings of the church in these two texts.

First, the church is a distinct people, a people with a different love, a different ethic, and a different hope. And in that sense the church is very definitely set apart in both Augustine and Yoder. And yet, for both, the church is not separate. The decision both theologians made to describe a realm with which the church could be identified but which was not limited to or synonymous with church is crucial. Not only are the heavenly city and the order of redemption communal realities which are not restricted to the church, both of the differing responses and loves which they instantiate will exist within each individual, as well. And it is crucial to both Augustine's and Yoder's models that the two cities or orders are intermingled during this present age. These distinctions between "the two," unlike many others which have been proposed by theologians in the centuries which divide Augustine and Yoder, are not made in order to establish a nonporous boundary between the church and some temporal/secular realm, either for the purpose of naming the "true" church or for the purpose of carving out differing spheres of authority. Instead, the distinction between "the two" serves to say that there are ways of living in the world which are ordered by the love of God and embrace of Christ's lordship, and there are ways of living in the world which are ordered by other loves and resistance to Christ's lordship.

Second, this distinctiveness which is not utter separation means that the church is socially and politically active, contributing to earthly justice and peace, while never confusing the justice and peace of which human governments are sometimes capable with the eternal and true justice and peace in which God created and to which God calls all creation. In Yoder's terms, the ethic of love will always be obscured, as if in a cloud, for those who do not recognize and dedicate themselves to the lordship of Jesus Christ. The church should call them ever closer to that reality, but the church also knows that all creation will not submit to it until the *eschaton*. In Augustine's terms, the city of God makes the most it can of the same goods used by the earthly city while they sojourn together, but in the *eschaton* the city of God will enter into true and ultimate peace while the earthly city will pass away.

Third, both have been unfairly accused by their critics of various forms of social fatalism. Augustine is said to be so pessimistic about the earthly city as to render social transformation a hopeless impossibility. Yoder is said to be so sectarian and idealistic about the church as to render social transformation irrelevant. In reality, both theologians were calling their audiences to reflect on the social optimism and triumphalism of their recent past, and to move forward with a more modest view of what can be achieved in the present age and how these achievements are not the center or meaning of history. Augustine wanted the church to remember that the Roman empire was not the center of history, and its failure was not a failure of God's redemptive purposes, which are the meaning of history. Yoder wanted the church to remember that the social optimism of the liberal Christianity of the late-nineteenth and early twentieth centuries had come unravelled, and that to advance a particular political platform was not to establish the kingdom on earth. This feature is well summarized in the following passage from Yoder, which is redolent with "Augustinian" political modesty:

> The Christian speaks not of how to describe, and then to seek to create the ideal society, but of how the state can best fulfil its responsibilities in a fallen society. The Christian witness will therefore always express itself in terms of specific criticisms, addressed to given injustices in a particular time and place, and specific suggestions for improvements to remedy the identified abuse. This does not mean that if the criticisms were heard and the suggestions put into practice, the Christian would be satisfied; rather, a new and more demanding set of criticisms and suggestions would then follow. There is no level of attainment to which a state could rise, beyond which the Christian critique would have nothing more to ask; such an ideal level would be none other than the kingdom of God.[20]

Fourth, there is the possibility of a further similarity which is not an explicit feature of either of these texts. I believe that if we take together the strengths of the proposals of the two cities and the two orders, they give us the very crucial ability to articulate how and why the church must be open to what God is doing and what Christians can learn from those who are outside the church. Seeing God's work in all the world, being open to God's action outside the church, and working together with people of other faiths or no faith clearly are not strong emphases in either of these texts. Yet the insistence in Augustine that both cities do the same things on earth

20. Yoder, *Christian Witness*, 32.

with the same goods, but do them with differing aims and purposes, creates an open space for moving in these directions. And the insistence in Yoder upon the lordship of Christ over all creation and all of life, and his recognition of the other realm as one of God's providence, point even more firmly toward receptiveness to God's presence in the world outside the church as well as cooperative witness in the world with those of other faiths.

Finally, from all of these similarities, another emerges, and one which raises the question of whether what we have been talking about all along was indeed a doctrine of the two, or if these are actually doctrines of the three. There is a third reality at play in the two cities and the two orders, a complex spatio-temporal reality best named by Augustine: the *saeculum*. It is the present time and space in which the two cities coexist in Augustine, which Yoder describes as a time and space in which some already order their lives in response to the lordship of Jesus while others do not yet recognize his lordship.

It is the *saeculum* which has informed the best attempts to offer constructive uses of "secularity" over-against "secularism"; and it is the *saeculum* which puts the lie to the idea of a "public square." There is no space which we can call "public" of which the church is not already a part, in which the church must struggle to find a voice or a role. Nor is there a "public square" which is the one spatial reality carved into separate spheres, one of which belongs to the church. Instead there are all those parts of creation which recognize, submit to, and point toward what is ultimate and true, and those parts of creation which do not see, choose not to submit to, or point away from what is ultimate and true; there are these two and there is the *saeculum*, the time and space during and in which these two coexist. During the *saeculum*, the role of the church is not translation into or correlation with the supposed "public"; it is the bold yet modest witness of a pilgrim community intent upon peace and justice, but without illusion that they can perfectly effect either.

CHAPTER 10

Heroes/Villains: Anabaptism and the Rise and Fall of Yoder in Political Theology (2019)

Among the religious Reformers of sixteenth-century Europe, the Anabaptists were viewed by Catholics and Protestants alike as having peculiarly dangerous approaches to theology and politics. Resonant with the peasant uprisings and calling for previously unimaginable settlements of church and governmental authorities, they were the targets of particular scorn and persecution. Thereafter, their tradition was little known to most Christians outside their own ranks, and considered particularly irrelevant in relation to politics. It is of special interest, therefore, that among the various approaches to political theology since its rise as an academic discipline in the twentieth century, Anabaptism has come to the forefront. In what follows, we will consider various faces and imaginaries of sixteenth-century and twentieth-century Anabaptisms.

SIXTEENTH-CENTURY ANABAPTISM: TWO THEOPOLITICAL PARADIGMS

Reformation historiography is notoriously contested. Most people who tell the stories of the Reformation have something to prove or disprove in the telling, even if unwittingly. Nowhere is this more true than in the historiography of the so-called "Radical Reformation." Who were the Anabaptists of the sixteenth century, why did they break from the other Reformers, and what did they believe? These questions are met with starkly differing answers depending on what the answerer wants to prove or disprove. It could be said that there are two particular, and particularly contrasting, narratives which are each taken as the paradigmatic tale of the radicalism of the radical wing of the Reformation.

One is the story of Münster. Münster is a city in Germany where, during the early 1530s, Reformation outcasts found refuge. Energized by the Peasant Revolt of 1525 they were agitating for economic and social change along with ecclesial reform. Among these were followers of Melchior Hoffman, who began as a lay preacher, traveling to spread the news of Luther's reforms. Hoffman's radical anti-clericalism, spiritualism, and visionary apocalypticism eventually led him to break with Luther. When he encountered Anabaptists in Strasbourg, he adopted some of their theology while also persuading some of the more spiritualist and apocalyptic members to adopt some of his. Hoffmann died in prison in Strasbourg, but some of his followers, the Melchiorites, expanded upon the theocratic element of his program, rejecting the disavowal of "the sword" common to many other Anabaptists.

A group of Melchiorites, led by Jan Matthijs and Jan van Leyden, seized control of Münster in 1534 and declared that all those refusing adult baptism would be expelled from the city. Münster became a magnet for persecuted radicals and was declared the New Jerusalem. A community of goods was established in which all things were shared in common, as in the Jerusalem church of the book of Acts. In most other respects, Israel of the Old Testament was the norm, including the reinstatement of polygamy. The message was spread that God was establishing the kingdom at Münster. Large numbers of radical Anabaptists tried to reach Münster from across Europe. Most were apprehended en route, and many of these were executed, but others reached New Jerusalem only to see it descend into war and tyranny. The bishop sent an army to besiege the city, and several leaders of Münster, including Jan Matthijs, were killed in their attempts to re-enact war narratives from Israel's history. Jan van Leyden was proclaimed "king of the New Zion" in 1534, and brutally suppressed all opposition to his reign. In June of 1535, the theocracy was defeated. Jan van Leyden and two of his fellow leaders were tortured and their mutilated bodies taken on tour before being returned to Münster and suspended in cages on the church tower. There the remains of the Anabaptists would stay as a warning against radicalism for generations to come.[1]

Although now empty, the three cages still hang high on St. Lambert's Church tower today. These cages image something of the paradigmatic place Münster came to hold in some historical imaginaries of the Reformation. For Protestants outside of Anabaptism, Luther, Calvin, and Zwingli (though all complicated characters in their own rights) are largely assumed to have had reasonable views on reformation, and (on the whole) to have acted reasonably in carrying them out. The "Radical Reformers," on the other hand, are thought to have taken it all too far, carried away by their extremist biblical and theological convictions.

However, there is a very different paradigmatic narrative which takes central place in sympathetic imaginaries of the Radical Reformation: the story of Dirk Willems. The Melchiorites were one branch of Hoffman's followers, but a very different branch of Anabaptists influenced by Hoffman arose in the Netherlands. In stark contrast to the revolutionary theocracy in Münster, Dutch Anabaptists coalesced around the pacifist separatism of Dirk Philips and Menno Simons, the man for whom the Mennonite churches would be named. The *Martyr's Mirror* tells the story of Dirk Willems, a Dutch Anabaptist who in 1569 was imprisoned, as were so many Anabaptists of the time. Knowing he faced certain death, Willems bravely escaped prison and ran for his freedom. His escape did not go unnoticed, however, and he was pursued. When Willems ran across frozen water, his pursuer followed but broke through the ice and was drowning. Knowing that his choices were either to save his own life and leave the man to die, or save the man's life and certainly forfeit his own, he turned back and pulled his pursuer from the icy water. He was in turn recaptured, imprisoned, and sentenced to death. He was burned alive, and accounts of the execution told of a horrible ordeal in which winds kept blowing the flames away from Willems, prolonging his torture before death.[2]

The story of Dirk Willems and images of the 1569 copper etching of his self-sacrificial rescue figure prominently in the self-understandings of many Anabaptists today. The narrative is also often cited by those from outside Anabaptism who come to appreciate the extent to which pacifist Anabaptists of the sixteenth century were hunted and brutally killed by

1. On Münster, see Krahn et al., "Münster Anabaptists"; Goertz, *Anabaptists*, 28–31.

2. Braght, *Martyrs Mirror*, 74.

Catholics and Protestants alike, yet did not abandon their commitment not only to refuse violence, but to actively love their enemies.

These two paradigmatic narratives image the assumptions and agendas behind most approaches to these sixteenth-century movements. The cages of Münster are the central image for approaches in which the Anabaptists were the slightly (or extremely) mad cousins of the Reformation, who are either easily dismissed from the narratives which "matter," or are focused upon as a peculiar curiosity. The etching of Willems with arms outstretched to his drowning captor is the central image for approaches in which the Anabaptists were the noble forbearers of an important tradition, redolent with unimpeachable integrity, whose narratives must be recaptured from those who have dismissed or misunderstood them. The Anabaptists are either the ultimate sinners or the ultimate saints of the Reformation, and nowhere more particularly than in their theopolitics.

Both violent theocratic radicalism and nonviolent communitarian separatism were real presences among sixteenth-century radical Reformers. Both the narratives of Münster and Willems capture something genuine about this wing of the Reformation. (Though the question may legitimately be raised: is there such a "wing" of the Reformation, or is this a categorical grab-bag into which are thrown all those who broke with both Rome and the Magisterial Reformers?) Good historiography is suspicious of such paradigmatic narratives, and also disavows any attempts to adjudicate between contested narrations of the Radical Reformation in terms of identifying the "true" Anabaptism. It would be equally foolhardy to try to identify *the* "true" political theology of sixteenth-century Anabaptism. However, we can say something of the *lasting* political theology of traditional Anabaptism.

Sixteenth-century Anabaptism has no document which, in the time itself, was what the *Ninety-Five Theses* were to Luther's reforms, or the *Thirty-Nine Articles* were to the English Reformation, or the *Institutes of the Christian Religion* were to Calvinism. There was no single defining moment, no one central leader, and no definitive systematic theology of Reformation-era Anabaptism. This was the case for several reasons. There were distinct origins of Swiss, German, and Dutch Anabaptisms, each region having its own Anabaptist leaders with differing emphases. These leaders and their communities were, in most places, so fiercely persecuted that they did not have the luxury (nor often sufficient lifespan) to write as prolifically or systematically as magisterial Reformers—though Dirk Philips and

Menno Simons came close. Furthermore, it is not clear that many Anabaptists would have wanted to write more systematically than they did, even given more amenable circumstances; their biblicism and primitivism did not inspire systematic doctrinal exposition. Subsequent generations of Anabaptists long remained content that their theology should be lived rather than systematized.

Nevertheless, one document which has been particularly widely (though by no means universally) embraced as a clear expression of "normative" Anabaptism by many of the Anabaptists who survived the Reformation and became the various Mennonite and Brethren traditions which remain intact today, is the Schleitheim Confession (or Schleitheim Brotherly Union). The document arose from a meeting within Swiss Anabaptism, shortly after their formal parting from magisterial Reformers led by Zwingli, and used a series of articles to describe "true" Anabaptism in contrast to other Reformers, and in response to Protestant and Catholic misunderstandings of Anabaptism, as well as in differentiation from other Anabaptist groups. The writing of the agreed articles has traditionally been attributed to Michael Sattler, a key Swiss Anabaptist leader. The subjects of the seven articles were baptism, the ban, breaking of bread, separation from evil, shepherds of the church, the sword, and swearing oaths. They expressed the distinctive Anabaptist practices of adult baptism and communion of believers thus baptized, as well as their distinctive views on separation from evil which necessitated the rejection of violent and coercive means ("the sword") and refusal to wield such means through political power, as well as the practice of "the ban" (the distinctively Anabaptist rendering of excommunication which focused on communal practice of Matt 18:15–17). To modern readers, "the ban" may seem harsh, legalistic, and authoritarian—a clear example of religious intolerance. Taken in context, however, it is a strikingly distinct practice of mutual admonition and potential reconciliation where other Christians were practicing violent persecution and torturous execution of those who strayed.

Undergirding all these articles is the conviction that the normativity of Jesus Christ requires of Christians a way of living in the world that is entirely distinct from standard human politics which depend upon violence, dominating exercise of authority, allegiance to powers other than God, and the absence of practices of reconciliation. This took different shapes in different Anabaptist works and communities, with differing degrees of separatism (not all Anabaptists embraced the thoroughgoing separatist dualism of Schleitheim). Yet the desire for utterly Christoform politics was a central and driving theopolitical conviction which set many Anabaptists apart, which made them seem particularly subversive and dangerous in the sixteenth century, and eventually particularly attractive in the twentieth century.

JOHN HOWARD YODER AND THE TWENTIETH-CENTURY RISE OF ANABAPTIST THEOPOLITICS

Due to the inattentive dismissal of Anabaptism by those outside the tradition, aided unwittingly by the historic insular sectarianism of most Anabaptist communities, it is not much of an exaggeration to say that the stories of Anabaptism were told almost entirely without sympathy outside of Anabaptist circles from the sixteenth through nineteenth centuries. It was not, in fact, until the late-twentieth century that Anabaptism began to claim both sympathetic and normative voices in Christianity beyond Anabaptist circles. Within a few decades, in the United States in particular, Anabaptism moved decisively out of the shadows, where it had been neglected and misrepresented, into the limelight, where it became positively fashionable. In the 1960s, it was still seen (if acknowledged as a living tradition beyond the "cultural" peculiarities of Amish communities) as the tradition of those who took things too far, and were isolated in their extremism. By the 1990s, it was a tradition which explicitly and decisively shaped the thought of the man many would consider the most influential theologian of the time, Stanley Hauerwas. The influence of Anabaptism was not only spreading among academic theologians; it was quickly gaining popular influence as well. In 1990, the popular evangelical magazine *Christianity Today* featured an article titled, "The Reformation Radicals Ride Again," showcasing the work of Hauerwas along with John Howard Yoder and James William McClendon Jr. It heralded Anabaptism's new day, saying, "Almost to the present day the Anabaptist vision has been written off as irrational or irrelevant or both. But that is changing."[3]

It is always overly simplistic to attribute a significant shift such as Anabaptism's unprecedented rise in prominence to the influence of a single individual. Other previously "sectarian" Christian groups moved into the Christian "mainstream" in the late-twentieth century, and there is no doubt that a complex mixture of social, cultural, philosophical, and political

3. Scriven, "Reformation Radicals Ride Again," 14.

trends contributed to Anabaptism's increased profile. However, it is also true that the work of John Howard Yoder played a crucial role.

Born in 1927 to a Mennonite family in Ohio, Yoder was raised in Mennonite communities and churches, and attended a Mennonite university. He then went to Europe, where he worked for the Mennonite Central Committee (MCC), studied under some of the most significant theologians of the day, including Oscar Cullmann and Karl Barth, and met his French-Mennonite wife, Anne, with whom he had seven children, one who died in infancy. He taught in the Associated Mennonite Biblical Seminaries in Indiana from 1960 to 1984, part-time from 1977 when he became a professor at Notre Dame, where he would teach until his death in 1997. His most well-known book is *The Politics of Jesus*, first published in 1972. His corpus is thoroughly occasional, comprised mostly of extended pamphlets (*The Christian Witness to the State, Nevertheless*) and collections of essays (*For the Nations, The Priestly Kingdom, The Royal Priesthood*).

Yoder's work faced two directions. Facing his fellow Mennonites, he encouraged a break with traditional sectarianism, inviting them into deeper ecumenical and wider social engagement. Facing non-Anabaptist Christianity, he insisted that Anabaptism was not an historical nor a cultural curiosity, but in fact the tradition in which some of what should have always been most central to Christianity had been preserved. Three features of Yoder's work are strongest in his legacy within political theology: his critique of "Constantinianism," his portrayal of the politics of Jesus, and the centrality of nonviolence.

Yoder's critique of "Constantinianism" was not only a rejection of the particular settlement enacted between the Roman empire and Christianity during the reign of Constantine, though it certainly included this. It was a much broader argument about different understandings of how the people of God relate to and wield power and sovereignty. Yoder argued for an understanding of the proper politics of the people of God as prophetic and exilic instead of established and settled. For Yoder, this contrast was a trajectory traceable through the histories of both Israel and the church. The writings of the Hebrew Scriptures coalesced around two tendencies: the ideal of Israel as a powerful monarchical kingdom settled in the land (the Davidic strand), and the ideal of Israel as a counter-witnessing, sojourning people with no king but YHWH (the "Jeremianic" strand). Yoder believed that the centrality of the counter-witness of the prophetic Jeremianic strand is attested by its existence in the canon; only the strongest convictions about the importance of this alternate narrative could have allowed it to be preserved alongside the official monarchic narrative. Israel in exile and diaspora becomes the normative Israel in this counternarrative. There is a recognition that YHWH never desired the people to have a king like other nations and warned them that monarchy would not go well for them (1 Sam 8), alongside a conviction that the sovereignty of YHWH is greater than the power of all earthly sovereigns.[4]

According to Yoder, the life and ministry, death and resurrection of Jesus Christ all point to the rejection of the Davidic interpretation in favor of the Jeremianic. Jesus redefined "king of Israel" in line with Isaiah's suffering servant instead of David's powerful successor. Jesus is, without doubt, a powerful king; but he redefines both power and kingship through suffering service, becoming the king who leads through serving and who demonstrates his power through dying. And the church is called, gathered, and commissioned by Jesus to reign and rule with him in this same way.

> Jesus made it clear that the nationalized hope of Israel had been a misunderstanding, and that God's true purpose was the creation of a new society, unidentifiable with any of the local, national, or ethnic solidarities of any time.[5]

The church is meant to be the space on earth in which the reign of Jesus Christ is visible, even though it will not be recognized by the world as either powerful or sovereign because the life of the church should be marked by nonviolence and servanthood. The church should live in the world as Jesus did, witnessing to the character of his reign. Like Israel, the church has had two competing narratives about settlement, establishment, and sovereignty, and just as the Davidic strand was the dominant and official narrative of Israel, Constantinianism has been the dominant and official narrative of the church, challenged by prophetic, exilic counternarratives throughout Christian history, particularly within Anabaptism.[6]

The Anabaptists are not unqualified heroes in Yoder's telling of this story, however. As with his entire corpus, there is an apology for the best of Anabaptism as well as an assessment of Anabaptism's failings. The apology is a call to emulate their exilic, countercultural resistance to dominant understandings and uses of power and sovereignty. The assessment of

4. Yoder, *Jewish-Christian Schism Revisited.*
5. Yoder, *Christian Witness to the State,* 10.
6. Yoder, *Preface to Theology; Royal Priesthood.*

Anabaptism's historical failings targets sectarianism: the church cannot be faithfully prophetic or exilic if it understands its distinctness in terms of absolute separation. One cannot "pray for the peace of the city" in which one is in exile without being actively a part of that city's life.

Yoder's portrayal of the politics of Jesus is a second, overlapping central theme. According to Yoder, when Jesus shunned the politics of Davidic monarchy, he did not shun politics *per se.* He rejected status quo politics, transcending standard options. When Jesus resists temptation in the desert, declares his "political platform" at Nazareth, feeds the multitudes, teaches about the coming kingdom, confronts the temple authorities, and submits to crucifixion, he is living and proclaiming this alternative politics. This was not the politics of the Zealots, calling for violent insurrection to throw off the Roman oppressors. Nor was it the politics of the Sadducees and Herodians, collaborating with Rome in order to be realistic. This was not the politics of the Essenes, withdrawing from society to form desert enclaves. Nor was it the politics of the Pharisees, remaining in society but withdrawing into separatist subcultures to maintain purity. The Gospels portray Jesus as constantly offered, and often tempted, by these options, only to reject them at every turn.[7]

Yoder related these options to the often assumed binary: one must either be "political," engaging with politics as they exist, or one must be "apolitical," withdrawing into a sectarian existence. The binary implies that the former is the responsible and realistic route while the latter is the irresponsible and consequently irrelevant route. Jesus, according to Yoder, resisted this binary as well as multiple ways of instantiating the "political" and "apolitical" choices offered to him. Instead, Jesus took a stand which was deeply political, but not aligned with any of these standard a/political options. And he gathered a countercultural community, the church, to become the bearer of this alternative politics in the world.

Again, the two-sided apology/assessment agenda of Yoder's work is clearly in evidence. To non-Anabaptists, this was a message that conceding to politics-as-usual is not the way of Jesus, and there is much to learn from Anabaptism's conviction that the entirety of the life and teachings of Jesus is normative for all of Christian life. To Anabaptists, the message was that withdrawal into apoliticism was not the way of Jesus either, and insofar as they had historically favored the purity of their witnessing communities over the faithfulness of their political engagement, they had also missed the

---

7. Yoder, *Politics of Jesus; For the Nations.*

point. In the following description of Jesus's politics, the two sides of the critique are both plain:

> He refused to concede that those in power represent an ideal, a logically proper, or even an empirically acceptable definition of what it means to be political. He did not say (as some sectarian pacifists or some pietists might), "you can have your politics and I shall do something else more important"; he said, "your definition of *polis*, of the social, of the wholeness of being human socially is perverted."[8]

One of the main features of this perversion, and the third central and overlapping theme, is violence. The politics of the status quo maintains and depends upon the necessity of violence, yet those who reject violence have too often opted for apoliticism instead of a politics transformed by nonviolence. The nonviolence of Jesus is neither the idealistic, humanist, nor the instrumental, pragmatic type of pacifism common in modernity; the argument is neither that we can convince everyone to be peaceful and end war on earth, nor that nonviolence is the best technique for getting important things done in the world. Instead the argument is that Christians must, like Jesus, renounce every claim to seize power over human events and make things turn out "right" through violence—a claim which would only properly belong to Jesus, if anyone, yet which he steadfastly refused, even unto death. This is not "pacifism" as a rule, much less as an instrument for political purposes. It is wholesale renunciation of "the compulsiveness of purpose that leads the strong to violate the dignity of others" in the pursuit of their ends (whether or not those ends be legitimate), as well as a renunciation "of our legitimate ends whenever they cannot be attained by legitimate means"; together these renunciations lead us into "participation in the triumphant suffering of the Lamb."[9] Again, this is both an apology for the preservation of Christian nonviolence in Anabaptism, as well as an assessment of how pacifism had taken forms within Anabaptism which were wrongly driven by legalism and/or concern for purity.

Yoder's work spoke a resoundingly clear word about and to Anabaptism, a word which was not easy for either audience to hear. As the popularity of his writings and his influence reached their peak, some wondered whether people were hearing just how difficult this word was. When editing a collection of essays by non-Anabaptists expressing appreciation

8. Yoder, *Christian Witness to the State*, 247–48.

9. Yoder, *Preface to Theology*, 248.

for Anabaptism, John D. Roth commented that their admiration was "a double-edged sword":

> On one hand, admiration from quarters that had once relegated Anabaptism to the scrap heap of theological history is a rather heady experience, evoking sentiments ranging from quiet gratitude to smug self-satisfaction. At the same time, however, the sectarian impulse to self-conscious hand-wringing, especially in the face of encomiums, is never far from the surface. Is such praise really merited? Are the essayists aware of the yawning gap between Anabaptist ecclesiology and the lived reality of many contemporary Mennonite congregations? Or in a slightly different vein, will the growing public affirmation of the Anabaptist tradition inevitably blunt its radical edge? Can one embrace Anabaptist–Mennonite themes of pacifism without a corporate memory of suffering? Does the growing impulse to frame Anabaptist–Mennonite theology in the systematic, highly self-conscious language of the academy inevitably attenuate a faith that is best expressed in daily discipleship and the lived experience of the community?[10]

ANABAPTIST THEOPOLITICAL LEGACY: TWENTY-FIRST CENTURY QUESTIONS

John Roth asked some important questions about the legacy of Anabaptism. At least two further critical questions must be added to his. The first follows on from his question about the pressing of Anabaptist theology into systematic, academic discourse. My question in particular is whether "Anabaptist political theology" is possible. I do not raise this question for the standard reasons others might, namely based either on the mistaken assumption that "sectarian" traditions such as Anabaptism are "apolitical," or the mistaken assertion that "sectarian" traditions have opted out of "responsible" public discourse and practice and are therefore irrelevant to genuine political theology. Anabaptism has never been apolitical, even in those times and places where Anabaptists considered themselves to be apolitical; Anabaptism has always enacted various alternative, often subversive politics with alternative, often subversive theories of Christian responsibility.

Some Anabaptists have recently embraced the label of "political theology." And certainly, given a very broad definition of "political theology," we can speak meaningfully of "Anabaptist political theologies." However, if we

10. Roth, *Engaging Anabaptism*, 13.

moved more specifically to the question of what the differences are between "ethics" and "political theology," we may find that the former sits far more comfortably within most Anabaptist frameworks than the latter.

Ted A. Smith has recently offered a compelling delineation of the differences between ethics, particularly in its modern instantiations, and political theology. He suggests that ethics is concerned with "moral obligations that play out within immanent networks of cause and effect." Although this "immanent frame" may be able to "accommodate many kinds of moral reasoning," focused on acts, consequences, or virtues, it cannot readily imagine, recognize, or accommodate that which exceeds the frame and/or is exceptional to it.[11] Smith understands the ethical as a valid and important way of reasoning, but also notes its significant limits, suggesting that we need theological ways of reasoning about politics which exceed these limits—that we need political theology. This is not about the superiority of one theological discipline over another, but about the limits of the ethical without the possibility of the theopolitical—theopolitics without attention to the ethical is likewise undesirable.

Interestingly, Smith identifies Yoder as one of the significant exceptions—as a theological ethicist who "offered visions that exceed this frame."[12] It may be that in this exceptional excess Yoder demonstrated the theopolitical strength of Anabaptism. It is certainly the case that the reductionist acts of "translation" from "theology" to "ethics," which are the mainstay of Protestant "social ethics," are practically nonsensical to Anabaptism, and this has surely been one reason among others for its rise in popularity alongside postliberalism. On the other hand, it may be that what was most truly exceptional and excessive (in this sense) in Yoder's thought was where he turned his critical gaze toward historical Anabaptism. His theological ethics was not only a rejection of modernist Protestant projects of "translation," it was a rejection of traditional Anabaptist moralist reductionism. And it could be argued that in this rejection he did not always himself succeed. Can Anabaptism speak beyond questions of what we should do and how we should live in relation to political realities and imperatives, into relentlessly metaphysical questions about the meaning of politics in the eschatological life of the Triune God? And can Anabaptism allow the latter questions and answers to trouble the former? Or will we

11. Smith, *Weird John Brown*, 5.
12. Smith, *Weird John Brown*, 5.

find, after Yoder, that Anabaptism is too thoroughly "ethical" to practice "political theology"?

This, however, is not the most pressing question about Anabaptist political theology after Yoder. Behind closed doors throughout most of his adult life, more publicly since his death, and particularly since 2013, questions and revelations about Yoder's conduct have been serious and persistent. It was widely known before his death that in the 1990s, Yoder had faced a disciplinary process within the Mennonite Church after accusations of sexual misconduct. However, this was often told as a tale of redemption—of Yoder's submission to discipline, the persistence of friends and colleagues who walked with him, and the tenacity of the loving disciplinary practices of Anabaptism.[13] At the writing of this chapter, the following could still be found on the Global Anabaptist Mennonite Encyclopedia Online:

> In 1991, eight women brought formal complaints of sexual misconduct against Yoder. As a result, Yoder's home congregation (Prairie Street Mennonite Church) appointed a task force to investigate the allegations. After a year of work, the task force concluded that "the charges brought by the women are accurate, and John has violated sexual boundaries." Moreover, said the official press release, Yoder "has acknowledged the truth of the charges and has expressed deep regret for the hurt his actions have caused for the women." On 27 June 1992 the Indiana–Michigan Conference of the Mennonite Church began a process of formally disciplining Yoder. Yoder submitted to this process, which would last a little over four years. As a part of the process, Yoder acted to cut off any ongoing relationships that were deemed inappropriate and agreed not to pursue any new ones. He also agreed to undergo therapy "to work thoroughly with the issues involved." In the summer of 1996 the discipline process concluded successfully, with the Church Life Commission and the Indiana–Michigan Mennonite Conference saying that they encouraged "Yoder and the church to use his gifts of writing and teaching." The semester before he died he once again taught a course at Associated Mennonite Biblical Seminary.[14]

13. This was the frame in which the story was perhaps most widely circulated, when published by Hauerwas in *Hannah's Child*. Hauerwas has since admitted his version of the story was wrong, because he "simply did not understand the extent of the activities," he "was too anxious to have John resume his place as one of the crucial theologians of our time," and he "did not appropriately acknowledge how destructive John's behaviour was for the women involved" (Hauerwas, "In Defence of 'Our Respectable Culture'").

14. Nation, "Yoder, John Howard (1927–1997)."

This straightforwardly redemptive framing of Yoder's story has been shattered. For many, his victims in particular, the frame never held. After heated conversations exploded across Mennonite websites throughout 2013, multiple official processes were launched to reconsider and address what Yoder had done and how Mennonite institutions had been involved.[15] Anabaptist Mennonite Biblical Seminary launched internal processes which led to a "Statement of Confession and Apology" as well as a "Statement of Commitment," both read as part of a public "Service of Lament, Confession, and Commitment." The Mennonite Church USA appointed a "Discernment Group on Sexual Abuse and the Church." As part of this process, a historian was given unprecedented access to previously secret and personal documents as well as opportunities to gather oral history through interviews. The resulting historical account calls into question every element of the redemptive version of events.[16]

"Eight women brought formal complaints" to the attention of local Mennonite church leaders in 1991, but Yoder's estimated actual victims include at least 50–100 women, abused on occasions across at least twenty years, and in countries spanning the globe. Yoder's "submission" to the disciplinary process was grudging, resistant, obfuscating, and defensive. Although he "agreed to undergo therapy," when the process resulted in a troubling psychiatric assessment, Yoder refused to acknowledge its findings and demanded that the report be repressed. The process did not "conclude successfully," but died a death of exhaustion and futility. It resulted in no formal apology from Yoder or the institutions where his abuse was well known. Although the possibility was raised, it resulted in no form of personal or institutional restitution to his victims. It resulted in no immediate changes of policies or structures. It does not appear that anything was accomplished other than Yoder's restored professional status.

In addition to all the standard reasons why powerful people are allowed by institutions of all sorts to continue abusing, a key reason why Yoder's abuse was so impervious to attempted rebuke and correction—no fewer than seven groups were assembled for these purposes by various Mennonite bodies between 1980 and 1997—was that he framed his abuse in terms of important advances in Christian ethics. Yoder claimed to believe in a new Christian path to be forged beyond puritanical views of sexuality,

15. At the writing of this chapter, the University of Notre Dame had not announced any such response. See Salgado, "Yoder Case Extends to Notre Dame."

16. Goosen, "Defanging the Beast."

and he portrayed himself explicitly to his employers, his victims, and any who questioned him, as engaging in "experiments" with his "sisters" in order to blaze a trail into truly Christ-like sexuality. Throughout most of his adult life, Yoder serially groomed women and initiated them into this "sisterhood," pressing them into his revolutionary sexual "therapy." The man who had made Anabaptist political theology generally, and Christian pacifism specifically, academically respectable and popularly appreciated lived a life of persistent and disturbing patterns of domination, manipulation, and violence in the name of extending the moral normativity of the way of Jesus beyond social ethics into sexual ethics.

In a piece of contemporary Anabaptist political theology which resists the ethical reductionism with which many Mennonite leaders who were aware of Yoder's abuse approached him (as if the problem was that he was breaching agreed moral frameworks and imperiling his marriage), Mennonite theologian Jamie Pitts[17] rightly identifies a more complex, less immanently framed "sexual politics" at work here. Using Pierre Bourdieu's concepts of "misrecognition" and "symbolic violence," Pitts has begun the work of critical political analysis of Yoder's published work in light of his abusive behavior and unpublished sexual "ethics."[18]

Will the unprecedented levels of sympathetic attention to Anabaptist traditions which followed Yoder's rise to prominence recede following the revelations and long overdue truth-telling about his life? It is striking to me that the crisis over Yoder's legacy, in some significant ways, brings us back to where we began. Assessments of contemporary Anabaptist political theology are not so far removed from the long centuries of binary historiography of sixteenth-century Anabaptism. As Yoder and Hauerwas rose to prominence, and Anabaptist communities became more visible and visibly engaged, the Anabaptists became, for many, the embodiment of what Christianity should be/come in the twentieth century. The spirit of Dirk Willems was alive and well on the pages of some of the most popular and influential theological texts of the day and in the newly noticed work of Anabaptist believers in organizations like Christian Peacemaker Teams. The Anabaptists were the theopolitical heroes of the day.

Those who opposed the rise of Anabaptism's popularity did not do so casually or with indifference; the opponents of Yoder and Hauerwas have

17. Jamie Pitts also read an early draft of this chapter. His comments and questions, for which I am most grateful, were indispensable.

18. Pitts, "Anabaptist Re-vision."

been vocal and fierce. They targeted Yoder's and Hauerwas's "Jesuology," ecclesiocentrism, and pacifism as irresponsibly extremist theology; this sort of extremism had been kept out of the mainstream all these centuries for good reason. And as Yoder's extreme failings as a Christian and a human being came undeniably into focus, those already prejudiced against the tradition were given the perfect fodder for their arguments against the irresponsible and unrealistic extremism of the ecclesially centered, nonviolent theopolitics he espoused. Not only has Yoder's nonviolence been disproved, but we now see clearly how idealistic pretensions to perfectionism mask the inevitable sinfulness and violence of those who propound it; once again the Anabaptist crowds followed and propped up a violent, extremist leader despite their peaceful teachings. Just as the critics suspected all along, the spirit of the leaders of Münster is alive and well, and the Anabaptists are the theopolitical villains of the day.

In our tellings of Reformation history and contemporary theology, Anabaptism is repeatedly pressed into hero or villain status. The truth, of course, is that Anabaptists were and are normal Christians and normal human beings, capable of and culpable for both sublime acts of love and peace and sinister acts of injustice and violence. There is a unique and particular call to an alternative, cruciform, nonviolent politics in the Anabaptist tradition, but there is no unique ability to fully and faithfully enact this politics within Anabaptist people—just as there is no unique ability to fully and faithfully enact the best impulses of liberal (or any other) theopolitics within the people who espouse them.

Perhaps one key to both the faithful enactment of the best of Anabaptism by contemporary Anabaptists, as well as to the hospitable interpretation of Anabaptism by contemporary non-Anabaptists, is whether and how we all attend to power. Along with Anabaptist discernment of the call to renounce dominant uses of power must come the discernment not shown by Yoder and many of those who surrounded him to critically analyze actual assertions of power from the highest level of politics all the way down to the most mundane interactions of everyday life. Likewise, as non-Anabaptist theologians consider the countercultural, subversive political message and lived experience of Anabaptist traditions, we must have the discernment neither to idealize nor villainize them so thoroughly that we lose sight of how *both* they and we are exercising power.

CHAPTER 11

Sixteenth-Century Theopolitics: A Sermon for the 500th Anniversary of the Reformation (2017)

What actually happened in the Reformation? The way some Protestant Christians talk about it, you would think that through the Reformation all that was most deeply wrong with the world was suddenly put to rights. The way some Catholic Christians talk about it, you would think that far from "reformation," these movements were the unravelling of everything right and good. The reality, obviously, must be something more complex than either of these estimations.

Likewise, the way some theologians talk about the Reformation, you would think that everything which occurred in Europe during the second half of the sixteenth century hinged entirely on matters of Christian doctrine. And the way some historians talk about the Reformation, you would think that those same events were entirely about the political upheavals of the dawning of early modernity. Again, the reality is something more complex than either of these characterizations.

The area in which I do most of my scholarly work is known as political theology, and it is a shared tenet of many in my field that the theological and the political are not, and indeed never have been, separable. This is not to say, of course, that institutions like churches and governments cannot be distinct or separate; they, of course, can be.

Rather the tenet is that when human beings deliberate about and enact structures through which common life, common obligations, and common aims are sought and shared, their assumptions and claims and outworkings are at once political and theological: political because they have to do with understandings and ordering of shared human lives and structures, and theological because they have to do with understandings and ordering of the meaning and purpose of shared human lives and the orientation and obligations of humans' ultimate allegiance. From this perspective, there is no point claiming the Reformation was *really* about theology, and no point claiming the Reformation was *really* about politics. It was theopolitical: impinging on and impinged upon by both the political and the theological at every level.

Martin Luther was, like any human, immersed in and motivated by both his deepest convictions and his social, cultural, and political context. In 1520, by which time it had become clear to him that his efforts to reform the church would soon lead to his excommunication from it, Luther wrote his *Appeal to the Christian Nobility of the German Nation*. In it, both convictional–doctrinal and pragmatic–political agendas are evident. If he was to part ways with Rome, he must begin to work out what the relationship between the authority of the church and the authority of secular rulers might be in the absence of centralized church authority in the papacy. At the same time, if he was to part ways with Rome, it was in his political interest to seek the support of the German princes and protection for his reformers.

In the *Appeal*, Luther introduced his doctrine of the priesthood of all believers. In place of the late-medieval understanding of one government with two estates (the temporal and the spiritual), he proposed that no group has exclusive claim to the spiritual estate because all Christians are consecrated as priests by baptism.[1] Going further, he argued that temporal power itself is likewise baptized and, he wrote, "we must allow it to be priest and bishop."[2] This argument served his dual purposes of raising a theological critique of church hierarchy and urging the German princes to seize their political power in relation to the papacy.

However, in his efforts to reject Roman hierarchy and to find favor instead with the German princes, Luther's proposal in effect stripped the church of all political significance. He wrote,

1. Luther, "Address to the Christian Nobility," 70.
2. Luther, "Address to the Christian Nobility," 70.

temporal power has been ordained by God for the punishment of the bad and the protection of the good, therefore we must let it do its duty throughout the whole Christian body, without respect of persons, whether it strikes popes, bishops, priests, monks, nuns, or whoever it may be.[3]

It was not long before the backpedalling began. When the Duke of Saxony banned Luther's New Testament, Luther wrote *On Secular Authority*,[4] and his tone changes dramatically; his deference for the princes turns to defiance. "[S]ince I was not afraid of their idol the pope when he threatened me with the loss of heaven and my soul," he wrote, "I must show the world that I am not afraid of the pope's lackeys either, who threaten me [only] with the loss of my life and worldly possessions."[5]

Here again we see both pressing political circumstance and earnest theological enquiry. On the one hand, Luther needs to articulate how and why legal action against his reforms is an overstepping of temporal authority. On the other hand, Luther has a theological interest in the tension between two strands within Scripture, represented by our two readings this evening from Genesis and Matthew (Gen 9:1–17; Matt 5:17–26). There is a strand which says that life should be taken from those who take life, and that God has given the power of the sword to temporal rulers in order to punish the guilty and protect the innocent. There is also a strand which says do not repay evil for evil, do not kill, turn the other cheek, love your enemies.

Luther wants to resolve this tension without denying the priesthood of all believers. Instead of distinguishing between persons hierarchically, dividing priests, monks, and nuns (who must reject violence and love their enemies) from us normal humans (who must be governed by an ethic of just retaliation), Luther resolves the tension by distinguishing arenas of authority instead: the kingdom of God and the kingdom of this world.

According to Luther, Christ rules over the kingdom of God, a spiritual kingdom of love, justice, and order, where there is no sin and no need for law, punishment, or violence. As ruler of this kingdom, Christ is the only authority over all that which is inward and spiritual. And if all were perfect Christians, this would be the all-encompassing reality. However, says Luther, all humans remain sinful, and thus there must be a kingdom of this

3. Luther, "Address to the Christian Nobility," 70.
4. Luther, "On Secular Authority," 3–43.
5. Luther, "On Secular Authority," 6.

world where temporal rulers wield the sword to maintain order. They have authority over outward and bodily matters pertaining to common life, but not over beliefs or spiritual matters which are ruled over by Christ alone.

This doctrine of the two kingdoms provided Luther with a new line of attack against Rome. He said, "They have managed to turn everything upside down: They ought to rule souls with God's Word, inwardly, and instead they rule castles, towns, countries and peoples, outwardly." Luther's doctrine also provided a call for restraint to the princes. He said, "And the secular lords, who should rule countries and peoples outwardly, do not do so either . . . they want to rule spiritually over souls, just as the spiritual authorities want to rule in a worldly manner."[6]

Although this doctrine would come to be understood as the center of Luther's political theology, Luther would soon change his views again. When faced with peasants' revolts, the rise of Anabaptism, and radical apocalyptic groups, he insisted upon the duty of temporal authorities to punish wrongdoing *including in spiritual matters,* insisting that these groups must be brutally suppressed. Among these groups which Luther opposed were the Anabaptist Christians who had parted company with Lutheran Reformers. Named for their practice of re-baptizing adults who had been given Catholic baptism as infants, the Anabaptists were imprisoned and executed by Protestants and Catholics alike. Yet, *they* categorically rejected any use of violence.

It is difficult to overemphasize the compelling peculiarity of this witness. Absolutely all European Christians at this time thought it was not only permissible but positively incumbent upon them to violently repress the teachings and practices of other Christians whom they opposed—but the Anabaptists did not. Where Luther had relegated the Christian ethic of enemy love and nonviolence to the kingdom of God, which governs the personal, spiritual life—leaving the ethic of violent retaliation intact in the outward kingdom of this world—the Anabaptists insisted that enemy love and non-retaliation must govern the entirety of the truly Christian life, and for this reason there must be clear and absolute separation between the Christian community and the governmental structures maintained through violence and force.

Ironically, contrary to contemporary narrations of the genesis of the modern, liberal state (in which the need for secular government arose in order to protect the political from the dangerous, violent threat of the

6. Luther, "On Secular Authority," 27.

theological), in fact, the earliest call for the separation of church from state came from Anabaptist Christians, who believed they must retrieve a way of nonviolent Christian life which must be separate from the dangerous dependence of earthly governments upon violence. This is a story most of us do not learn in school or even in university, although we may very likely learn, in some form, the story of Martin Luther and his Reformation.

Wherever we each find ourselves standing now in relation to the Reformation: Christians who feel strongly invested in evaluations of either its theological success or wrongheadedness; or outsiders to Christianity who are either fascinated by Reformation politics or repulsed by its violence; it is likely that we would all do well to complexify our narrations of this watershed era. When we assume neat and tidy compartmentalizations of the theological and the political, whether through narrating Reformation history as *either* theology *or* politics, or through understandings such as Luther's two kingdoms which attempt to narrate *human existence* in terms of the inwardly private theological and the outwardly public political, we ignore the actual outworkings of theopolitics—for good or ill.

And we are more likely to ignore the potential witness of those who trespass our conceptual boundaries in unexpected ways, like the Anabaptists and their witness to the possibility of a theopolitics of nonviolence—a witness to the possibility of a way of peace in this world not through the protection of the political from the theological, but through a theopolitical rejection of the violence of politics-as-usual.

Amen.

IV. Apocalyptic: Hope in Narrations of Suffering and Violence

Narrating Catastrophe, Cultivating Hope: Apocalyptic Practices and Theological Virtue (2018)

As 2017 draws near its end, it is difficult to imagine that many of us will be feeling particularly full of hope. Political and natural catastrophe seems to have been mounting, now surrounding and nearly overwhelming us. I will always remember an interaction in the first week of this year as emblematic of the hopeless mood in which we find ourselves. I was at the till in the Marks and Spencer food hall in central Cambridge—not exactly in the epicenter of any of the world's suffering, of which there is too much and from which I remain too sheltered. As my transaction drew to a close, I said to the clerk, "Thank you. Happy new year!" He barely looked up from the till as he spat back, "Yeah, what are the chances?!"

I understood him entirely, but also felt something remarkable was happening if, even in this incredibly comfortable little corner apart from it all, polite public conversation was now marked by such despair. And yet, in what can now only seem an act of providential irony, the theme of our 2017 SSCE Conference was hope. Where could we possibly begin? Perhaps it was this conundrum of having to address so unlikely a theme that drove me to such an unlikely beginning point for a discussion of hope: apocalyptic.

My consideration of apocalyptic and hope will proceed in four parts. First, I will briefly describe the sort of theological virtue framework within which I hope to place the following discussion of apocalyptic. Second, I will describe apocalyptic as a narration of catastrophe which opens the door to hope. In the third part, I will seek to begin bringing these discussions of virtue, apocalyptic, and hope into contemporary relevance by delving into narrations of one of the greatest moral catastrophes of our day. Finally, I will begin to gesture toward a Christian apocalyptic practice for cultivating hope in relation to this and indeed every catastrophe.

Embodied Rationality of Hope: Theological Virtue in Herbert McCabe

My approach to this exploration into apocalyptic and hope is from within the framework of theological virtue ethics. My main interlocutor in sketching this framework will be Herbert McCabe, chosen rather than the usual exponents of Christian virtue because of the emphasis in his work on the inextricably bodily and political nature of all human knowing and being, and the irreducibly radical nature of the Christian moral life. Critics of virtue who continue to misunderstand it as a discourse that is necessarily conservative and/or inwardly focused (either in terms of internal disposition of the individual alone, or in terms of in-group communitarianism) would do well to attend to McCabe's work.[1] McCabe was thoroughly Aristotelian, thoroughly Thomist, and thoroughly Wittgensteinian.

As an Aristotelian, he emphasized the "ineluctably political" nature of humans.[2] He rejected modern conceptions of society as the product of many individuals and argued instead for the social production of the individual.[3] As a Wittgensteinian, he argued that society was constituted linguistically.[4] For the individual in the human community, said McCabe, "language and rationality, the symbols in which she can represent herself to herself—are precisely what makes possible her specially human kind of

1. I am indebted to supervisions with a recent master's student, Thea Reimer, whose explorations into McCabe's anti-dualism prompted me to use him as primary interlocutor.

2. McCabe, *Good Life*, 25.

3. McCabe, *Good Life*, 26. McCabe emphasizes that the community does not over-determine the individual, even though it constitutes us: "while political or social communities constitute us rather in the way the biological species does, we also creatively respond to and modify them. Indeed, the linguistic community just is a community of such responsive and creative animals" (*Good Life*, 34).

4. McCabe, *Good Life*, 26.

individuality."[5] Along with Wittgenstein McCabe also emphasized that human rationality is not internal or private. He wrote,

> It was, I think, the greatest achievement of Wittgenstein to show that the mental world is not private. To have a mind is not essentially to have a means of withdrawing from the public world into a secret world of your own, it is to have a special way of belonging to the public world, it is to belong to a community.[6]

McCabe took this line further, emphasizing that linguistic rationality is not only irreducibly social and political, it is irreducibly bodily; as he put it, it is "a material business, a matter of this human body among others."[7] In contrast to the multiple philosophies which assume a self or mind that is somehow different from the body, and is the real center of human moral agency, McCabe insisted that the "human body is the source of significant moral behavior. The body is not, like a knife or a word, significant because it is used in a certain way; the body is not used, it uses these other things."[8] Like many twentieth-century virtue ethicists, McCabe also highlighted the narrative form of human rationality and morality. He argued that "[h]uman living is enacted narrative."[9]

As a Thomist, at the forefront of a version of Thomism which McCabe himself did not call by that name, he understood the moral life in these social, embodied, linguistic, narrative terms as also irreducibly theological. While all human living is enacted narrative, and this is true at various levels in relation to various kinds of narrative, Christians understand this primarily in relation to the narrative of Jesus Christ. McCabe wrote that "just as our human life consists in enacted narrative so our divine life is just our participation in the enacted narrative of God. The revelation of God to us is nothing except our being taken up into that narrative, the human story that

---

5. McCabe, *Good Life*, 27. McCabe's description of human rationality and morality is, in my view, too focused on distinguishing human animals from non-human animals; such claims continue to be weakened by our growing understanding of the capacities and experiences of other animals. However, for our purposes, it is also important that McCabe's arguments about humans do not stand or fall on these contrasts with other animals; they serve in his argument as illustrations rather than points of logical progression.

6. McCabe, "Validity of Absolutes."

7. McCabe, *Good Life*, 31.

8. McCabe, "Validity of Absolutes."

9. McCabe, *Good Life*, 71.

is the sacrament or image of the unseen and unseeable, incomprehensible God."[10]

McCabe defined virtue as "dispositions to enter into community, not to be absorbed in some lifeless way by a collective, but to develop those specifically symbolic, linguistic, rational relationships with others which we can sum up in the word 'friendship' and which are characteristic of groupings of human animals."[11] And in the case of the church, these symbolic, linguistic friendships are specifically sacramental. For McCabe this meant drawing constantly from both past and future in order to envision the moral life of the present.

> [T]hose who share sacramentally in the language of the future form a community or, better, a movement within the world . . . that seeks the bearing of the future on the present. The discoveries of the church about the moral life are the result of a communal exploration, an exploration that has been going on with many set-backs and side-trackings for centuries . . . The Christian moral outlook is essentially drawn from our [historical and present] contact with the future. It is based upon the virtue of hope.[12]

When pointing toward the virtue of hope, it will have been Aquinas' account which McCabe had in mind. According to Aquinas, hope is both a natural passion shared by all animals, human and non-human, which fixes our attention on a future possible good and enables us to strive toward it,[13] and a theological virtue, which fixes our attention ultimately on God, and what is desirable and possible because of God—which for Aquinas, of course, is nothing less than eternal beatitude.[14] As a theological virtue, hope is accompanied by faith and love, and stands between them. Aquinas says that faith begets hope and hope begets love.[15] Faith is an intellective power,

10. McCabe, *Good Life*, 77–78. Note that McCabe is careful here to say that God is not a story and God does not have a story, as God has neither beginning nor end; rather, the incarnate life of Jesus Christ becomes the human story which is to us sacrament and image of the God who cannot be contained in a story.

11. McCabe, *Good Life*, 29.

12. McCabe, *Law, Love and Language*, 154.

13. Aquinas defends the existence of hope in non-human animals in *Summa Theologiae* I–II.40.3.

14. Aquinas argues that hope is a virtue and that it is proper to hope for eternal beatitude in *Summa Theologiae* II–II.17.2-3.

15. Aquinas, *Summa Theologiae* I–II.40.7. See also *Summa Theologiae* II–II.17.5–8 on the relation of hope to the other theological virtues.

and hope is an appetitive power. That is, faith receives knowledge of God and the good from God, which funds the drive of hope to move us toward our ultimate future union with God. By faith we know that for which we should and can hope, and as we journey, hope allows us to see God not only as the end for which we strive, but the help which makes our striving fruitful. Hope could be relegated to some very personal, individual, realm of disposition were it not for the fact that it is as directly connected to love as it is to faith. Faith informs and funds hope; hope stretches outward and is extended in love.[16]

As a virtue, hope is the rightful ordering and orientation of the passion of hope, and the vices which name its disordering are despair and presumption. As a theological virtue, hope cannot be described as the mean between these two vices. Aquinas explains that a theological virtue, infused in us as it is from God and having God as its rightful object, does not consist in a mean because there can be no extremity; we cannot have too much faith, hope, or love.[17] So while despair is a lack of hope, presumption is not an excess of hope but rather hope wrongly orientated.

In this brief sketch of McCabe, we begin to see a theory of *virtue*, *community*, and *practice* which insists upon an understanding of human rationality and Christian morality as always already *political, linguistic, narrative, bodily*, and *sacramental*. This is the moral framework that I am bringing to bear in the following consideration of apocalyptic, in which I construct an account of how apocalyptic can point us toward practices which cultivate the infused virtue of hope.

Practising Apocalypse: Speaking the Unspeakable

In his characteristically wide-ranging and insightful book, *Hope without Optimism*, Terry Eagleton contrasts the hope which he commends with both "leftist historicism," which theorizes an ever-improving trajectory and ultimate socialist culmination within history, and "sheer apocalypticism," in which, as he puts it, "the transformative event erupts unpredictably into a degenerate history in which there is little to be valued, and can find no grounding there." He finds these options "equally implausible," arguing that

16. Aquinas, *Summa Theologiae* II II.17.2 and II II.17.8.ad 2.
17. Aquinas, *Summa Theologiae* II–II.17.5.

while the former trusts too much in history (is too optimistic), the latter sees too little value within history.[18]

Eagleton is correct about "apocalyptic*ism*," a term that can encompass a wide variety of worldviews and ideologies which interpret human life in relation to an expected, usually imminent cataclysmic event culminating in the end of the world and its history, and the beginning of a new utopian reality. Such views are usually accompanied by convictions that those who expect and understand the coming cataclysm will be on the right side of events and vindicated in the new utopia, while others will plumb the depths of previously unknown human suffering and be vanquished. Taken in this sense, apocalypticism is routinely rejected and denounced by Christian theologians and ethicists as a world-devaluing, history-denying, morally dualistic framework—and rightly so. However, although this is a fair condemnation of various forms of apocalypticism, we must not read this backwards onto the ancient genre of apocalyptic. These features are neither particularly representative of the apocalyptic genre, nor is such apocalypticism peculiarly related to those with apocalyptic sacred texts.

As John Collins has noted, the end of the world was not a consistent feature of apocalyptic texts, nor in any way particularly associated with apocalypse.[19] Apocalyptic is not a genre about the imminent end of the world in a battle between the forces of good and evil; rather, Collins argues, it is about "[t]he dissonance between the belief in the supremacy of YHWH and the actual political order," explored in a way that "enables people to dissent from a culture that they find oppressive or otherwise unacceptable, when they lack the practical means to change it," thus serving as an "expression of power on the part of the powerless."[20]

One point to be made here, which has been the focus of previous arguments I have made about the normativity of apocalyptic, is that what is central to apocalyptic—indeed, what makes something an apocalypse—is not cataclysm but unveiling, "an imaginative vision of the future which functions to jolt us out of our status-quo perceptions and see current social reality for what it truly is in relation to God."[21] Here I want to build upon this understanding of apocalyptic while also considering more closely the

18. Eagleton, *Hope without Optimism,* 37–38.

19. Collins, *Apocalypse, Prophecy, and Pseudepigraphy,* 34. See also 37.

20. Collins, *Apocalypse, Prophecy, and Pseudepigraphy,* 323.

21. Phillips, *Political Theology,* 148.

darkness of apocalyptic—how and why an apocalypse does often narrate catastrophic events.

Even those who are aware of the scholarly consensus on apocalyptic as a literature of dissent from and re-envisioning of socio-political powers in the face of oppression—those who do not operate under the misconception that apocalyptic is the battle of Armageddon in Revelation—may still misunderstand the genre as escapist fantasy which serves only to soothe the mind of the oppressed community. However, an important recent work on apocalyptic argues instead that the earliest known Jewish apocalypses cultivated active resistance.

In *Apocalypse against Empire*, Anathea Portier-Young describes Daniel, the Apocalypse of Weeks, and the Book of Dreams—the earliest extant historical apocalypses—as prophetic visions which interpreted past, present, and future in terms of the limited, transitory nature of temporal powers, providing a counter-discourse to the imperial discourses and practices of domination and hegemony. Crucially, she argues that this counter-discourse not only offered a different interpretation of empire, it also called for and cultivated practices of resistance. In fact, she concludes that the interrelation of vision and praxis resistant to empire formed the heart of early Jewish apocalyptic:

> Apocalyptic faith maintained that what could be seen on the surface told only part of the story. It looked as if Antiochus would destroy God's people, the covenant, holiness itself. It looked as if empire wielded power over life and death. A people with open eyes could look through and beyond appearances to perceive the order of all creation and the enduring rule of God. They could name the violence and deception of imperial domination and hegemony, but also see in history a pattern for deliverance to come . . . they could behold a future for humankind, Jerusalem and Judea, earth and heaven, marked by justice, righteousness, and joy.[22]

While acknowledging the potential anachronism in her use of "domination" and "hegemony" as key categories for analyzing the socio-political realities of the authors and audiences of early apocalyptic, Portier-Young uses these constructs sensitively in order to highlight the ways in which the Seleucid empire subordinated and controlled its subjects. She argues that through strategies of domination ("social and ideological structures that create and maintain conditions of subordination" and "coercive forms of social control

---

22. Portier-Young, *Apocalypse against Empire*, 389.

as torture, execution, enslavement, plunder, policing, and military occupation") and hegemony ("nonviolent forms of control exercised through cultural institutions, systems of patronage, and the structured practices of everyday life"), the empire sought to control and discipline both the bodies and the imaginations of its subjects. It was these institutions, systems, and structures of imperial control that were questioned and resisted in apocalyptic. In particular, she argues, the language and symbols of apocalyptic enabled readers to reframe reality beyond the hegemonic constructs of the empire through revelations of divine providence and action, as well as to respond actively to this new, resistant framing vision.[23] Apocalyptic produced new vision, interpretation, and modes of resistant praxis.

Most of her argument is made through detailed historical work, but in one chapter Portier-Young also draws on trauma theory to analyze the experiences and responses of the communities from which these apocalyptic texts arose. Portier-Young describes how victims of trauma, whether individual or socio-political, struggle to find hope because of how we process traumatic memory.

In her landmark work on trauma, psychiatrist Judith Herman argued that the common experience of sufferers of trauma is the helplessness and terror which results when ordinary human responses to danger are of no avail. Danger triggers a complex of physical and psychological responses, giving the person in danger heightened senses, attention, emotion, and physical ability. Trauma arises when a horrific event occurs and danger mechanisms are engaged, but they can in no way stop or ameliorate the event. As a result, everything happening in the body that is meant to help a person resist, flee from, or intervene in the horror cannot serve its purpose, but instead "tends to persist in an altered and exaggerated state long after the actual danger is over."[24] The heightened state of danger preparedness persists, but in fragmented ways, resulting in the three main symptoms of post-traumatic disorders: hyperarousal, constriction, and intrusion.[25]

Hyperarousal refers to a sense of "permanent alert," a constant state of heightened awareness and/or vigilance in which people are easily triggered, irritated, or provoked, and which usually prevents good sleep.[26] Constriction is something like the other side of the same coin to hyperarousal; it

23. Portier-Young, *Apocalypse against Empire*, 383–84.

24. Herman, *Trauma and Recovery*, 34.

25. Herman, *Trauma and Recovery*, 35.

26. Herman, *Trauma and Recovery*, 35.

involves the sufferer lapsing into states of numb disconnectedness from their surroundings. Just as hyperarousal is a continued reliving of the heightened vigilance of the danger response, constriction is a continued reliving of the state of surrender into which victims of trauma retreat—a psychological flight when there can be no fight. It is easy to see how a life lived alternating between these two states, continuously feeling the moment of trauma both physically and emotionally, could become debilitating. But these experiences are further exacerbated by the fact that they are usually dissociated from what we might consider "normal" memory of the traumatic event.

Memories of trauma are usually experienced as "intrusion," the third major symptom. For the traumatized, spontaneous intrusions of memory which feel alarmingly like the original traumatic event break into both sleeping and waking consciousness. Herman says, "Long after the danger is past, traumatized people relive the event as though it were continually recurring in the present."[27] The reason why these memories erupt in such disturbing and visceral ways, and why they can be connected to, yet dissociated from, the experiences of hyperarousal and constriction is because we do not store memories of trauma the same way in which we store most memories.

Most memories are encoded linguistically and narratively; they become stories that can be narrated, and which form a part of our larger stories. Traumatic memories, however, "lack verbal narrative and context; rather, they are encoded in the form of vivid sensations and images."[28] Bessel van der Kolk describes how infants process information and experience through senses and movement, then develop the ability to process information and experience iconically (perceiving and storing images), then finally develop symbolic and linguistic schemata through which information and experiences are understood and stored in memory. During trauma, confronted with events that confound our established schemata, our symbolic and linguistic coding fails us and our central nervous systems revert to sensory and iconic memory.[29]

This prevents traumatic events from taking narrative form in the sufferer's memory, which might lend itself to trajectories of explanation, integration, or resolution. They cannot narrate their trauma, but they continue

27. Herman, *Trauma and Recovery*, 37.
28. Herman, *Trauma and Recovery*, 38.
29. Kolk, "Trauma Spectrum."

to feel its sensations and see its images. These isolating experiences of embodied memory function to call into question one's own sense of identity as well as one's sense of what orders the world, and it is posited that the repetition of these iconic memories continues to retraumatize victims until they are helped to reframe the memory linguistically.[30] Some trauma theorists are primarily interested in therapeutic methods for individual sufferers, and others focus on socio-political trauma and state terror; the importance of the victim's narration of trauma is theorized as equally important for individual and community alike. As Judith Herman puts it, "Remembering and telling the truth about terrible events are prerequisites both for the restoration of the social order and for the healing of individual victims."[31] She describes events leading to traumatic disorders as socially "unspeakable," and because we dare not speak them they emerge as a set of symptoms instead of as verbal narratives.[32]

Whether we are talking about an individual suffering a trauma like rape, or a society suffering a trauma like war—or, most likely of all, the complex interrelation of socio-political and individual trauma—traumatized people are cut off from their history and unable to relate it rationally to the present or the future until they are able to remember and narrate their history linguistically.

Herman posits three stages to trauma recovery: establishing safety, remembrance and mourning, and reconnection with ordinary life. During the remembrance and mourning stage, she explains, it is crucial both for memories of the trauma to take linguistic and narrative shape, usually in some process of writing and revising texts, and to mourn the loss contained in this newly narrated memory. However, trauma recovery does not end with narrating and mourning; rather, it is through narration and mourning that victims can reconnect with life in ways that include becoming empowered to resist and transform the realities surrounding the trauma.[33]

For Portier-Young, trauma theory helps us understand apocalyptic texts as interventions into the experiences of imperial terror which would have acted as a "rupture in time" if not communally narrated. Trauma, including the trauma of imperial domination, stops time. As Portier-Young

---

30. Herman, *Trauma and Recovery*, 39. Here Herman is also drawing on Horowitz, *Stress Response Syndromes*, 93–94.

31. Herman, *Trauma and Recovery*, 1.

32. Herman, *Trauma and Recovery*, 1.

33. Herman, *Trauma and Recovery*, chs. 8–10.

puts it, "Past and future recede, such that victims of trauma may become disconnected from their history and unable to formulate hope" for the future.[34] With this in mind, we can see the function of apocalyptic in terms of "reconnecting past, present and future so that their audiences can reclaim their history and self and move forward again in hope." Thus, the disturbing images of apocalypse are none other than the iconic images of traumatic memory, now being re-narrated in relation to "even more powerful iconic images of the ordered and ordering presence, reality, and activity of God."[35] Portier-Young argues that these apocalyptic narrations

> name confusion while opening the way for new understanding. They transform memory and relocate their individual and collective audience within the story of God's provident care. Through the story and witness of the historical apocalypses, individual and community receive back language, time, and meaning, along with a new vision and possibility of hope . . . In these ways apocalypse intervened in the logic of terror and so countered the empire's deadliest weapon.[36]

Seen in this light, the narration of monstrous powers and their destruction in apocalyptic texts functions not as a simplistic, dualistic worldview of good versus evil in a fantasy of the future, but rather as a way of both lamenting and understanding loss and oppression, and asserting that it is not the final word.

Lament—or in psychological terms, mourning—figures prominently in Portier-Young's analysis of apocalyptic and in Herman's discussion of trauma recovery. Like apocalyptic, lament can be understood as something that serves only therapeutically, to soothe the suffering and give them a sense of being heard. Emmanuel Katongole, however, argues that "lament is agency." Exploring both biblical lament and the lived experiences of contemporary Christian activists in East Africa, Katongole argues that the function of lament is in no way limited to the therapeutic, and instead "deepens and intensifies engagement with the world of suffering. Lament invites us into deeper political engagement, while at the same time reframing and reconstituting the very nature and meaning of politics."[37] He concludes of the activists he describes, for whom lament was a central practice:

34. Portier-Young, *Apocalypse against Empire*, 173.

35. Portier-Young, *Apocalypse against Empire*, 174.

36. Portier-Young, *Apocalypse against Empire*, 174–75.

37. Katongole, *Born from Lament*, 261.

They are not simply calling for law and order, nor simply for some justice and reconciliation. They would not be satisfied with mere legal and administrative adjustments within the framework of the current politics. They have been led to—and they invoke—a totally new vision of society. Their advocacy and initiatives reflect the shape of the world as both a radical critique of and an alternative politics to the politics of military alliances and economic greed. The faith activists understand themselves as both the agents and fruits of that new world.[38]

Important connections can also be drawn here between the functions of apocalyptic, lament, and tragedy. Rowan Williams argues that tragedy is a mode of representing suffering and loss, narrating trauma ritually in a way that is meaning-making for society, and which refuses passivity or resignation to suffering.[39]

Like lament and apocalyptic, tragedy can be misunderstood as a preoccupation with hopelessness. Williams argues, however, that "the tragic imagination" is not "a despairing vision of the cosmos or even a convention of contemplating the disasters that overtake great and powerful figures"; rather, it is "a particular kind of imagining that stays with the risk of returning to familiar and apparently resolved narratives of suffering and pacification and asking them new questions by finding new voices in which to tell or, better, realize the stories."[40] There are striking parallels between Williams's description of tragedy and trauma theorists' emphasis on narration as key to reintegration of sensory, iconic, and linguistic memory: "'the tragic' is originally a function of how a verbal and visual representation works in the mind of a community gathered to celebrate or affirm its resilience and legitimacy in full awareness of the fragility that always pervades its life."[41] Crucially, in Williams's view, tragedy arose as a form of communal liturgy, an "ordered affirmation of community" which, he says—and here his description resonates particularly with apocalyptic—"has something to do with the breaking-in of energy beyond the resources of the world as we know it."[42]

---

38. Katongole, *Born from Lament*, 262–63.
39. Williams, *Tragic Imagination*.
40. Williams, *Tragic Imagination*, 10.
41. Williams, *Tragic Imagination*, 10.
42. Williams, *Tragic Imagination*, 11.

Just as Williams discusses both the particular genre of tragedy and something wider arising from it, which he calls the tragic imagination, I am seeking to draw from the particular genre of apocalyptic, understood in new ways through the insights of trauma theory, a wider sense of what we might call the apocalyptic imagination—or better, apocalyptic imagination and praxis. Apocalyptic imagination and praxis

- express the power of those who have been rendered powerless and give voice to those who have been rendered voiceless;

- narrate catastrophe communally so that it can become part of a wider story within God's story instead of a device for re-traumatizing and oppression;

- mourn and lament the loss and suffering which are part of that narration;

- reveal the pretensions of oppressive powers to be false in light of God's providence, and the dominating hegemonic practices and discourses of oppressive powers to be deceptive and temporary;

- resist the temporal fragmentation of oppression by reclaiming history in order to better understand the present and provide hope for the future;

- and move narrators and hearers alike to actively resist domination, oppression, and false claims to power which belongs to God alone.

This proposal for an understanding of apocalyptic imagination and praxis connects at every point with the theological-ethical framework with which we began with help from McCabe: it emphasizes the integration of the political, linguistic, narrative, and bodily essence of our human nature and morality.

Concluding our discussion of apocalyptic here would allow us to end on a somewhat hopeful note about the nature and potential power of what might otherwise be a confusing textual genre with no obvious connection to Christian ethics. However, we should not be content to leave this exploration of apocalyptic either in the ancient past of its writing or at the theoretical level of this interpretation of apocalyptic in relation to virtue ethics and trauma theory. Instead, this interpretation of apocalyptic compels us to press forward and speak some unspeakable truths, and begin to grasp for ways to re-narrate one of our world's greatest, and frankly most hopeless, catastrophes: the catastrophic constructs and structures of racism.

HOPE AGAINST HOPE: BLACK THEOLOGY AND AFRO-PESSIMISM

It would not begin to be possible for me, within this scope and genre, to narrate the catastrophic global history of race. What I would like to do instead, because Black theologians in America have been speaking these unspeakable truths most clearly and unflinchingly for several decades now, is to narrate briefly the rise of and some significant shifts within Black theology in order to bring into relief the depth and breadth of the problem of race, as well as to raise the question of whether and how we can have hope for a future beyond this catastrophe.

Vincent Lloyd has argued that we have now seen three generations of Black theology in America.[43] The rise of the first generation was concurrent with the rise of "Blackness"—Americans of African descent refusing the labels of Negro and n****r given them by their white oppressors, and embracing their identity as Black. However, as Lloyd notes, for both the proponents of Black Power and the first generation of Black theologians, "Blackness was more than an identity in need of affirmation. Blackness was a privileged mode of existence."[44] To do theology as a Black man—and in the first generation, it was all about men—was not only to speak of God from the experience of Blackness; it was also to assert the "ontological symbol" of Blackness.

First and foremost in this generation of Black theologians was James Cone, who wrote that, "In Christ, God enters human affairs and takes sides with the oppressed. Their suffering becomes his; their despair, divine despair. Through Christ the poor man is offered freedom now to rebel against that which makes him other than human."[45] Thus, Cone argued that Blackness is "the primary mode of God's presence."[46] This claim is specifically Christological for Cone, and without implying anything literal about the color of his flesh, Cone argued emphatically that Jesus was Black. He believed that a Black theology of liberation must begin with the experience of Black persons in the world. Part of the failure of academic theology up to that point had been the failure to recognize that such theology was unwittingly drawn from the source of the experiences of, and thus served the

43. Lloyd, "Afro-Pessimism and Christian Hope," 191–205.

44. Lloyd, "Afro-Pessimism and Christian Hope," 192.

45. Cone, *Black Theology and Black Power*, 36. Cone first published this book in 1969, before Gutiérrez published *A Theology of Liberation*. His point may seem commonplace to us now, but Cone was at the forefront of such liberationist readings.

46. Cone, *Black Theology and Black Power*, vii.

purposes of, Whiteness.[47] Christian theology had ceased to be Christian theology and had become instead White theology. Naming and exposing White theology would be one of the central tasks of the first generation of Black theology.

According to Lloyd, the shift which characterized the second generation of Black theology, including a shift within the work of Cone himself, was moving the emphasis "from politics to culture, from struggle against oppression to embrace of African American history and values."[48] This shift also involved a move from emphasis on Blackness as *the* category of "the least of these," and *the* site of God's action, to a broader acknowledgement of difference and oppression, partially motivated by critiques of the sexism of the first generation which, in speaking from "Black" experience, spoke resolutely and unwittingly from black *male* experience. Lloyd describes this shift as a coming-to-terms with the fact that "a theology built on any particular 'least of these' elides the internal differences and complications within the group to which that name refers."[49] We could say that the first generation embarked on a project of protest, and the second generation moved toward a project of context (and, indeed, the phrase "contextual theology" arose in this period).

Lloyd identifies the central marker of the third generation of Black theology as a shift toward engagement with what wider Black Studies theorists have called "Afro-pessimism," a term coined by African-American Studies scholar, Frank Wilderson.[50] Afro-pessimism claims that "difference" elides the nature of Blackness, which cannot be reduced to an analogous category to differences in ethnicity, gender, sexuality, or dis/ability. Blackness is ontological because it names the non-being ascribed to Black persons. This ontology is inextricably woven into the deepest, most central fabric of Western metaphysics. The oppression of Blacks includes empirical conditions such as slavery and segregation, but those are the surface structures of a much deeper malady which cannot be addressed by reducing suffering alone. "Altogether," says Lloyd, "Afro-pessimism is so labelled because it points to the depth and gravity of Black oppression, and it suggests that the

47. See especially Cone, *God of the Oppressed*.
48. Lloyd, "Afro-Pessimism and Christian Hope," 194.
49. Lloyd, "Afro-Pessimism and Christian Hope."
50. See Wilderson, *Red, White, and Black*.

many efforts at ameliorating that oppression over the years, and decades, have been in vain."[51]

Where the first generation called for Blacks to seize their own liberation, and the second generation called for everyone to embrace difference and cultural particularity, the third generation says the work to be done—if indeed there is anything that can be done—is far deeper and more complex than either of these projects began to imagine. As Lloyd summarizes, "if the first wave of Black theology was political and the second wave was cultural, the third wave is metaphysical, though the metaphysics at stake have clear and powerful political implications."[52]

One of the most important works in this mode is J. Kameron Carter's *Race: A Theological Account*. Carter argues that Christian theology was an easy bedfellow to the philosophical and political processes by which humans came to be understood racially, and that theology itself was transformed in these same processes, "giving itself over to the discursive enterprise of helping to racially constitute the modern world as we have come to know it."[53] Carter shares with Afro-pessimism the conviction that race is a problem inscribed in Western metaphysics, and he adds to this a specific diagnosis of the modern "theological problem of whiteness," noting that "the politics of race and the politics of the modern state are of a piece, for both are religious or pseudotheological in character."[54]

The heart of the problem of race, as Carter understands it, is supersessionist. He describes it as "the problem of how Christianity and Western civilization became thoroughly linked with each other, a problem linked to the severance of Christianity from its Jewish roots." Thus severed from Judaism, Carter argues, Christianity "was remade into the cultural property of the West, the religious basis for justifying the colonial conquest" of the fifteenth to nineteenth centuries and "a vehicle for the religious articulation of whiteness." Modern political power came to be articulated in terms that were both religious and racial, "imagining certain bodies as obedient bodies and other bodies as bodies to be obeyed."[55]

---

51. Lloyd, "Afro-Pessimism and Christian Hope," 195. Key sources for Afro-pessimism broadly speaking include Franz Fanon, Sylvia Wynter, Hortense Spillers, and Achille Mbembe.

52. Lloyd, "Afro-Pessimism and Christian Hope," 197.

53. Carter, *Race*, 3.

54. Carter, *Race*, 40.

55. Carter, *Race*, 229–30.

In one chapter, Carter closely analyzes the work of Immanuel Kant, arguing that his vision of Enlightenment was an indelibly racial vision in which the particularity of Black and Jewish flesh is overcome by the universalism and rationality of whiteness which points toward the universal *telos* of humanity in which inferior, non-white peoples will cease to exist as humanity reaches its perfection.[56] For Carter, Kant's racist theopolitics is both the fruition of the colonial vision and the Christian supersessionist vision which were well established before him, as well as the setting of the stage of modern philosophy and politics to come after him—a philosophy and politics which Christian theology would continue to trade in (both intentionally and unwittingly) until it was interrogated by Black theology.

However, Black theology is not the hero in Carter's narrative. Instead, he critiques what Lloyd has identified as the first two generations, exemplified by James Cone, for trying to "salvage the blackness that modernity has constructed by converting it into a site of cultural power," a project that is "not radical enough" because "it ironically leaves whiteness in place." According to Carter, Cone rightly claimed that "the humanity that God assumes in Christ is specifically Jewish," yet this concrete, historical claim is undone by Cone's employment of Heidegger, via Paul Tillich, in which, "Oppression results from privileging a given history within being as the dominant or unifying narrative of the history of being as such" and "resistance can only be maintained from what itself is a nonhistorical, existential moment." This line of reasoning drives Cone back to a kind of supersessionism in which, as Carter puts it, "the limit that the Jewishness of Jesus represents is overcome by the 'more than' of the cross-resurrection event. This event universalizes the particular so as to broaden its reach beyond the Jews, their history, and their God."[57]

This line of reasoning also leads Cone to employ Martin Buber's concept of the I–Thou relationship, casting the struggle for Black liberation as a struggle to transform the White–Black, I–it relationship to a White–Black, I–Thou relationship. Carter insists "this is really only a settlement with whiteness, not its overcoming"; "I-ness itself functions as the normalizing term of the polarity."[58] Furthermore, Carter argues, "This problem dogs

---

56. See Carter, *Race*, ch. 2, where he draws particularly on Kant's *Anthropology from a Pragmatic Point of View*; "Of the Different Human Races"; and *Religion and Rational Theology*.

57. Carter, *Race*, 169–73.

58. Carter, *Race*, 190.

black theology because its liberation formulation of I-ness and Thou-ness, where Thou-ness itself is simply I-ness considered from the side of the object, has not broken far enough away" from all that which it sought to overcome.[59]

Carter does not end there: a considerable portion of his book is his constructive theological argument in response to his critical analysis in the mode of Afro-pessimism. However, in offering this short introduction to Carter's argument, I do not wish to move too easily forward into constructive proposals. We should not, after such a brief engagement with Afro-pessimism, be able to draw our considerations toward any sense of closure. The claims of Afro-pessimism are nothing less than devastating: for centuries our Western imaginations and societies have been formed at their very core around not just ideas of white supremacy—as if that were not sinister and devastating enough—but around a totalizing metaphysic, the ontology of which ultimately attributes being to whiteness and non-being to blackness. Our Christian faith has been formed at its very core around the rejection of particular, racial flesh in favor of abstracted, disembodied, universalizing understandings of salvation and human destiny which joined hand in hand with the ideology of whiteness.

It has been necessary and right and good that for two centuries now courageous women and men have fought to end the Atlantic slave trade, to end Black slavery and segregation in America, and Apartheid in South Africa, and that courageous women and men fight on today to redress all the related and attending structures of racism in our societies. And yet we see all around us—and let us be clear that it is all around us and not an exclusively American problem—the utter tenacity and resilience of the racist imagination. We have been chipping away—yes, sometimes in glorious moments of demolition, but nonetheless chipping away—at the tip of the iceberg. Whatever confidence we have had in our progress toward equality has rarely been grounded in hope; it has been presumption.

Honest engagement with Afro-pessimism necessarily tempts the reader to despair. And yet, despair is as vicious as presumption. We must cultivate hope—while agreeing with Eagleton that ours is a hope without optimism. Is it possible, then, for apocalyptic imagination and praxis to help us cultivate hope? Can we engage in practices of narrating this catastrophe which call into question the dominating and hegemonic discourses of race, making room for lament and mourning, so that we can resist our

59. Carter, *Race*, 190.

fragmented misunderstanding of our history, present and future, and re-claim them through both fresh understanding and renewed active resis-tance? Within the confines of this argument, I can only begin to gesture toward an answer: I argue that—although this description can by no means encompass all that the Eucharist is and does—we can properly consider the Eucharist just such an apocalyptic practice.

EUCHARIST AS APOCALYPTIC PRACTICE OF HOPE

In the constructive portion of his argument, J. Kameron Carter proposes "an understanding of Christian existence grounded in the Jewish, nonracial flesh of Jesus and thus as an articulation of the *covenantal* life of Israel"[60]—an understanding that locates what is ultimate neither in a racial distinc-tion nor in a universal absence of difference, but in covenant with the God of Israel, embodied in Jesus Christ. While Carter does not connect this to eucharistic practice, the Eucharist is precisely the place where we proclaim and receive the flesh and the blood of the covenant, where we proclaim and enact that in the death of that particular body, each of our particular bodies are incorporated into the one body which, as a covenantal body, is universal but not universalizing.

We have seen how the practices of apocalyptic, lament, and tragedy narrate catastrophe in ways that reconnect past, present, and future, and which depend upon divine intervention to place the present in proper per-spective in relation to God's eternal providence. These aspects of what I am calling apocalyptic imagination and praxis arise too when Rowan Williams argues that the eucharistic liturgy functions much like ancient tragic liturgy. In tragedy, Williams argues, "Once the civic discourse has been dismantled in the experience of catastrophe, it is then re-founded by the divine an-nouncement of a new state of recognition and justice, by the declaration that the violent rivalry which controls itself by finding scapegoats has been definitively refused and supplanted."[61] In the Eucharist, through dramatic narration of the Last Supper, we join in solidarity with those for whom the arrest and death of Jesus were a catastrophic dissolution and betrayal of communal and political life. We mourn, lament, and repent with the first disciples, and we receive the divine declaration of the justice established by the willing death which definitively supplanted the violent domination of

60. Carter, *Race*, 192.

61. Williams, *Tragic Imagination*, 126.

an empire over its subjects, of the twisting of religious power over prophets, and of sin and death over all creation. In the moment of eucharistic narration, every catastrophic rupture in time is healed as, in Christ, past, present, and future are reconnected in a trajectory of hope. And just as the ancients returned again and again to the familiar liturgies of tragedy, we continue this dramatic re-narration:

> We are made aware of the continuity of divine promise, and aware also, at every stage, of that which, on the human side, breaks the effect of divine promise. We continue to expose ourselves to hearing because we shall never have heard enough; having heard, we typically revert to un-hearing and un-seeing, and so must repeat endlessly the story of divine constancy and human infidelity.[62]

In our repetition of divine constancy made flesh and blood to us in Jesus Christ and in the sacrament of his presence, we also repeat the endless story of human infidelity. Insofar as Christian practice of the Eucharist has not functioned and does not function apocalyptically in relation to racism, this is an indication of our own failure to hear, receive, and enact the Eucharist's apocalyptic dismantling of the constructs and structures of race. We are like the Corinthians to whom Paul wrote, whose practice of the Eucharist failed to enact the dismantling of socio-economic divisions, and to whom he said, "all who eat and drink without discerning the body, eat and drink judgment against themselves" (1 Cor 11:29 NRSV).

In the Eucharist, a vision is opened to us—if we will see and receive it—of how the depth of catastrophic human oppression is met and overcome by what Herbert McCabe called the "revolutionary depth" of our future in God and how it impinges on our present life:

> The sacramental life as a whole, centering on the eucharist is an articulation both of human life now in its real but only dimly discernible revolutionary depth and of the world to come. It is only by the utter openness implied in faith that the revelation of this depth and this future can be received. It is because the sacramental life of the church is an entry into the deep meaning of human existence—an entry which is not merely a theoretical study but an actual encounter with the future reality that lies at the heart of human meaning—that it makes us able to take human behaviour seriously.[63]

62. Williams, *Tragic Imagination*, 125.

63. McCabe, *Law, Love and Language*, 145.

Appeals to the Eucharist such as the one I am making here tend to fall into one of two ditches, if not both. On the one side is the ditch of Eucharist as moral magic, which seems to suggest that our participation in the sacrament can in some unspecified way make us more moral and make social ills disappear. On the other side is the ditch of utter incredulity that we should make moral appeals to the Eucharist, which seems to suggest that good moral reasoning and argument cannot begin or end here but must immediately point us toward something more "practical." Here too McCabe is instructive when he relates the sacraments to the moral life in a way that avoids both magical and ineffectual misrenderings of Eucharist:

> The sacraments function in our moral life neither by giving us the extra will-power needed to keep in line with a moral code, nor by providing a pattern of life from which such a code might be theoretically deduced. They function more as does the experience of literature or drama: providing us with an insight, (but a uniquely authentic insight) into the nature and destiny of [humanity].[64]

In the Eucharist, we proclaim and are drawn into the uniquely authentic insight of human nature as non-racial and covenantal. The Eucharist is not a universalizing move away from the particular, but a being taken up into the incarnation; that story of the particular Jewish man, Jesus of Nazareth, who is sacrament of the God who dared to enter into but cannot be contained in human narrative. The drama enacted in the Eucharist is the drama of humanity being taken up into the story of the past, present, and future of God's covenant with Israel. This insight into our true nature and destiny is uniquely authentic because it is not only a story we tell or re-enact; it is the very presence of God with us through the body and blood of Jesus Christ in which we participate.

This participation in God's life is our hope. But it is not an easy hope, an optimistic hope which should lull us into a sense that a cup and a wafer can magic away racism, because in the Eucharist we also proclaim that our hope, and the life to which we have committed ourselves in its pursuit, is a dangerous, deadly business.

64. McCabe, *Law, Love and Language*, 145–46.

CHAPTER 13

Glimpses: A Sermon in Preparation for Lent (2015)

Both of our readings (2 Kgs 2:1–12; Mark 9:2–9) tell startling stories in which the curtains of heaven are opened ever so slightly and a glimpse of heavenly transcendence rushes into earth, momentarily lifting witnesses out of their normal existence, then departing just as quickly as it came. Elisha witnesses a glimpse of heaven in the ascension of Elijah. As he watches, heaven appears on earth for a brief moment as a fiery chariot and a rushing whirlwind. Elijah is swept up, and he disappears along with the glimpse of heaven. And the disciples witness a glimpse of heaven in the transfiguration of Jesus. As they look on, heaven appears on earth as a transforming cloud. For a brief moment, the disciples see Jesus as if in heaven, clothed in dazzling garments and surrounded by those who have gone before. Then suddenly the cloud, the prophets, and the glimpse of heaven are gone.

These two stories become bound up with one another in Christian Scripture, as Elijah appears with the transfigured Jesus. And as they descend the mountain, the disciples ask Jesus, "Why do the scribes say that Elijah must come first?" (meaning before the messianic age). In some ways, each of these two stories is unique in the role it plays in the history of Israel and the narration of the life of Christ. However, these stories by no means stand alone as unique glimpses of heavenly transcendence. Whether in the form of visitations or visions, such glimpses of heaven play consistently central roles in biblical narratives: angels visit Abraham, a burning bush confronts Moses, Isaiah sees God enthroned in the temple, Ezekiel sees dry bones becoming people, a sheet holding animals descends from heaven before Peter, a blinding light converts Saul, and John receives a whole book's worth of heavenly revelations.

But how do these glimpses of a heavenly transcendent realm shape the ways humans live in the world? Are earthly lives enriched or impoverished by heavenly visions and visitations? Many people, both atheists and Christians, believe that narratives in which humans glimpse heaven make us unfit for life on earth. For some of these heaven-skeptics, the main concern is living life to the full. People cannot fully live in the here and now when they are deluded with visions of a great beyond where they will someday find their future home, and people should not be encouraged to locate what is ultimately good outside of this world and outside of the time in which we live, where it is always out of reach.

For other heaven-skeptics, the main concern is oppression. Heavenly transcendence has often been used by Christians to encourage the patient endurance of oppression here and now because we have these glimpses of a realm in which suffering will end. Thus visions of a utopian realm which we will join in the future only serve to perpetuate the injustices of the present.

For still other heaven-skeptics, the main concern is moral dualism: us-and-them mentalities of right and wrong. Narratives of the coming-close of a time and place where good and evil are utterly clear allow people to identify themselves with the good, and to identify their enemies with evil, which will be defeated.

The heaven-skeptics make some good points, and their skepticism arises from ways in which narratives of glimpses of heaven have been used in genuinely terrible ways. But we can listen to these cautions against misuse without agreeing that glimpses of heaven on earth will and must always be used in these ways. How might these glimpses of heaven equip us for, instead of distracting us from, faithful living in the here and now?

To answer this, I think we need to turn to the very glimpses of heaven which heaven-skeptics often find most objectionable: the apocalyptic. Apocalyptic visions, seen most clearly in the Bible in the books of Daniel and Revelation, are those in which a heavenly figure reveals to a human a glimpse of realities which are future and transcendent, yet which are directly related to here and now. These texts were written in and for oppressed and persecuted communities who needed reassurance beyond all visible circumstances that God was still in control of human history, and who needed resources for questioning the power claims of their oppressors.

Their visions often included the future, dramatic toppling of those oppressive powers. They functioned to jolt people momentarily out of perceptions which seemed inescapable so that they could see that their circumstances were not final inevitabilities nor ultimate realities. Persecuted Jews and Christians were given, through these glimpses of heaven, the ability to stand before their oppressors and say, "You do not determine the unfolding of human history, and our destiny does not rest in your hands."

The Transfiguration, of course, is a very different sort of glimpse of heaven. Where the apocalyptic texts mainly functioned in relation to contemporary political powers, this glimpse of heaven primarily functioned in relation to contemporary discussions of the identity of Jesus. Yet we see a similar function in both: *the glimpse of heaven is a jolt which can shake people out of their status quo perceptions and open up possibilities for seeing what is ultimate in new ways.* The Transfiguration was a glimpse of heaven which opened up the possibility of seeing a reality which the disciples had just barely begun to dare to imagine: that Jesus was the son of God.

In all the synoptic Gospels, the Transfiguration is framed by the same series of events: Jesus tells his disciples that he is going to die, and that if they want to follow him they have to follow him to the cross; Jesus, Peter, James, and John climb a mountain together where Jesus is transfigured; they go down from the mountain and find the other disciples incapable of casting a demon out of a little boy, whom a frustrated Jesus readily heals; the disciples are amazed by Jesus and he immediately tells them again that he is going to suffer and die. Even though these stories come long before the passion narratives, through these declarations of Jesus, the Transfiguration is framed by the passion. Taken out of this context, the Transfiguration seems to be, straightforwardly, a decisive revelation of the divinity of Jesus. And it is certainly that. Through this glimpse of heaven, Peter, James, and John have their eyes opened anew to the reality of Jesus as the Son of God.

The placement of the Transfiguration in the Gospels, as well as the liturgical marking of the Transfiguration immediately before Lent, can also open *our* eyes anew, as it gives us the opportunity to see how the divinity of Jesus and his passion are inseparable from one another. Jesus told his disciples, "I am going to suffer and die, and you must be willing to suffer and die with me." They thought, "Hmm. That's odd. Whatever could he mean?" A thundering voice out of heaven says, "This is my beloved son. Listen to him!" And Jesus says, "I am going to suffer and die." *We cannot understand how God has come near to us in Jesus apart from his suffering and death.*

We have little glimpses of heaven before us just now. There is an inscription in the South Aisle[1] from Revelation: "I beheld and lo a great multitude which no man could number of all nations and kindreds and people and tongues stood before the throne and before the Lamb clothed with white robes and palms in their hands and cried with a loud voice saying, 'Salvation to our God which sitteth upon the throne and unto the Lamb.' Alleluia. Alleluia."

There is a glimpse of heaven which jolts us out of our routine perceptions: all peoples of the world gathered in worship around—of all things—a slaughtered and enthroned lamb. Slaughtered and enthroned. Passion and divinity interpreting one another. The one who is worthy, the one who gathers us, the one who was transfigured, the one who is ascended and glorified *is* the one who bears even in his resurrected, glorified body the marks of his suffering and death—as we see in the little glimpse of heaven depicted here above us, where the enthroned Christ reaches out to us with wounded hands.

As a community, we find ourselves now in a fairly profound moment of uncertainty. I find that this time every year tends to be one of personal uncertainty for many of us, which seems to arise because it is both an odd moment in the academic year, as well as a time when we feel the toll taken on us by the months of winter's darkness. And this year we have particular reasons to feel uncertain and unsettled. Who will our new principal be? What will happen to ministerial education in the Church of England? What is our role in the whole host of sweeping changes currently under debate?

Because of these unsettled uncertainties, I am thankful that Lent begins next week. I find Lent to be the most clarifying season of the Christian year, and I wonder if that is because it is the season in which the divinity and the passion of Christ most clearly interpret one another, and we are invited to understand ourselves anew in light of both his divinity and his passion in profound ways. And so my prayer for us during Lent is for glimpses of heaven. These may not be such dramatic ones; Elijah may not be involved. But I pray that they may jolt us out of our status quo perceptions of one another, of our community here, of our church, of "leadership," so that we may see all these things anew in the light of the mutually interpreting divinity and passion of Jesus Christ. And that in this light we may

1. This sermon was delivered in All Saints Church, Cambridge, which is adjacent to Westcott House. Photographs of the church and its inscriptions can be found at https://www.visitchurches.org.uk/visit/church-listing/all-saints-cambridge.html.

be reoriented and equipped anew for the lives we are called to live in this world, here and now.

In the name of the Father, and of the Son, and of the Holy Spirit. Amen.

CHAPTER 14

Penetrating the Surface of Reality: A Sermon
on Flannery O'Connor for All Hallows' Eve (2016)

Flannery O'Connor was a twentieth-century Southern American Catholic
Christian, and an author of novels and short stories. She was born in the
Southern state of Georgia in 1925. Her family and her early education were
devoutly Catholic. After graduating from Georgia's state college for women,
she joined the postgraduate writing program at the State University of Iowa,
where she became versed in William Faulkner, James Joyce, Franz Kafka,
T. S. Eliot, and the New Criticism, while also continuing to attend Mass
daily. She lived briefly in New York, but she could not abide the city. She
rented a flat in Connecticut attached to the home of a couple who would
become her literary editors and executors. She wrote her first novel in their
happy company. She then returned to Georgia, writing her second novel
and numerous short stories in the family home—a relatively modest farm
with a grand name: Andalusia.

If you are unfamiliar with Flannery O'Connor's work, you may be for-
given if, on the one hand, the idea of twentieth-century fiction inspired by
Christian convictions puts you in mind of C. S. Lewis's fanciful, adventur-
ous, and allegorical novels; or if, on the other hand, the idea of American
Christian fiction puts you in mind of saccharine sweet morality tales, utterly
devoid of irony or complexity. Flannery O'Connor's work, however, could
not more resolutely confound either sort of expectation. She and her work

were not only American, they were deeply Southern; she and her work were not only Christian, they were deeply Catholic. And for O'Connor, writing Catholic fiction in the mid-century American South meant writing something altogether startling.

In fact, her stories more closely resemble the horror genre in which some of us may be indulging to mark Halloween than they do the genres which we might read to our children at bedtime. Her stories are shocking, sometimes revolting, drenched in ironic and tragic violence and death. Like horror stories, her narratives often turn on shocking scenes for which the reader could not have been prepared: a grandmother is shot point blank; a disabled child is intentionally drowned; two upstanding citizens choose not to intervene, watching coldly as a migrant worker is killed by a tractor; a little boy hangs himself in an effort to meet his dead mother. Yet O'Connor's work is not horror, which uses the grotesque to thrill and entertain. Rather, her work employs the grotesque to enable perception of what is most deeply true of both humanity and divinity.

In 1955, she corresponded about a recent review in the *New Yorker* which called her new short-story collection "brutal and sarcastic." She said, "The stories are hard but they are hard because there is nothing harder or less sentimental than Christian realism. . . . when I see these stories described as horror stories I am always amused because the reviewer always has hold of the wrong horror."[1] For Flannery O'Connor, true horror was located in the nihilism of modern life—a nihilism which is so normal and comfortable that she believed something like the grotesque must be employed to reveal its horror. She said,

> The novelist with Christian concerns will find in modern life distortions which are repugnant to him, and his problem will be to make these appear as distortions to an audience which is used to seeing them as natural; and he may well be forced to take ever more violent means to get his vision across to this hostile audience. When you can assume that your audience holds the same beliefs you do, you can relax a little and use more normal means of talking to it; when you have to assume that it does not, then you have to make your vision apparent by shock—to the hard of hearing you shout, and for the almost-blind you draw large and startling figures.[2]

1. O'Connor, *Collected Works*, 942.
2. O'Connor, *Collected Works*, 805–6.

A cursory reading of her fiction, full as it is of tragically flawed fundamentalist Christians, can lead to the assumption that as a highly educated Catholic who had sojourned in the Northeast, she was lambasting the ignorant fundamentalism surrounding her in rural Georgia. However, more attentive reading soon makes clear that the fundamentalists are her allies; she values their edgy if misguided zeal, and they help her shout for the hard of hearing and draw startling figures for the almost blind. Her target is not fundamentalism, but the morally stultifying practical nihilism of both bourgeois Protestantism and intellectual atheism. Alongside the raging fundamentalists of her stories are the explicitly unbelieving intellectual types and the respectably religious types who do not genuinely believe anything. When the paths of these various characters cross, something joltingly terrible often ensues.

On the one hand, lazy bourgeois Protestantism has no time for suffering; on the other hand, intellectual atheism says that there can be no such thing as a good God because there is so much suffering. Neither are able to hold together the mysterious and painful yet liberating gospel of God who in Christ Jesus entered into human suffering and took it upon himself. Flannery O'Connor's stories did not preach this gospel; instead they sought to jolt readers out of the stupor of their nihilism and point them toward the gospel's sacramentality—the mysterious presence of the empowering grace of God in our normal material existence.

Flannery O'Connor believed that only bad religious fiction seeks to display convictions through arranging characters and events into "satisfying patterns." She said that more faithfully Christian fiction arises from sacramental theology; the novel, she said "must penetrate the natural human world as it is."[3] The jolting and often violent culminations of her stories were penetrations of the world as it is and preparations for receiving grace in the midst of that world.[4] Sometimes the moment of grace is refused, sometimes embraced, most often it seems to be planted like a seed, the fruition or death of which is left unknown, beyond the narrative.

This deep sense of the real presence of God's grace within all the material and complicated, bright and dark corners of human experience was central not only to O'Connor's work, but to her own short life. At the age of twenty-five, when Flannery O'Connor's career was just taking off up north and she felt she had found her home among like-minded people, she began

3. O'Connor, *Mystery and Manners*, 163.

4. O'Connor, *Mystery and Manners*, 112.

suffering chronic pain and was diagnosed with the same severe form of lu-
pus which had killed her father when she was fifteen. Her return to Georgia
from Connecticut was not willing; it was forced upon her by the fact that
her disease made it impossible to live independently. Most of her startling
tales of sacramental grace in the midst of acute human suffering arose from
over a decade of torturous personal suffering, from which she died when
she was just thirty-nine.

Flannery O'Connor wrote the way she did because she believed that
this was where her identity as believer and her identity as novelist were intertwined. Because, she said, the believer and the novelist share "a distrust
of the abstract" and "a desire *to penetrate the surface of reality and to find
in each thing the spirit which makes it itself and holds the world together.*"[5]

---

5. O'Connor, *Mystery and Manners*, 168; emphasis mine.

Bibliography

Adams, Nicholas, and Charles Elliott. "Ethnography Is Dogmatics: Making Description Central to Systematic Theology." *Scottish Journal of Theology* 53, no. 3 (2000) 339–64.

Aquinas, Thomas. *Political Writings*. Edited and translated by R.W. Dyson. Cambridge: Cambridge University Press, 2002.

Ariel, Yaakov. *On Behalf of Israel: American Fundamentalist Attitudes Toward Jews, Judaism, and Zionism, 1865–1945*. New York: Carlson, 1991.

Balmer, Randall. *Mine Eyes Have Seen the Glory: A Journey into the Evangelical Subculture in America*. 3rd ed. New York: Oxford University Press, 2000.

Bell, Daniel M. "State and Civil Society." In *The Blackwell Companion to Political Theology*, edited by Peter Scott and William T. Cavanaugh, 423–38. London: Blackwell, 2004.

Booker, Richard. *Blow the Trumpet in Zion: The Dramatic Story of God's Covenant Plan for Israel Including their Past Glory and Suffering, Present Crisis, and Future Hope*. Shippensburg: Destiny Image, 1985.

Boyer, Paul. *When Time Shall Be No More*. Cambridge: Harvard University Press, 1992.

Braght, Thieleman van, ed. *The Bloody Theatre or Martyrs Mirror of the Defenseless Christians*. Translated by Joseph F. Sohm. Scottdale: Herald, 1938.

Brown, Delwin. *Converging on Culture*. Oxford: Oxford University Press, 2001.

Brueggemann, Walter. *Genesis*. Louisville: Westminster John Knox, 1982.

Cameron, Helen, et al. *Studying Local Churches: A Handbook*. London: SCM, 2005.

Campbell, Douglas A. *The Deliverance of God: An Apocalyptic Rereading of Justification in Paul*. Grand Rapids: Eerdmans, 2009.

Carter, Craig. *The Politics of the Cross: The Theology and Social Ethics of John Howard Yoder*. Grand Rapids: Brazos, 2001.

Carter, J. Kameron. *Race: A Theological Account*. Oxford: Oxford University Press, 2008.

Cavanaugh, William T. "From One City to Two: Christian Reimagining of Political Space." In *Migrations of the Holy: God, State, and the Political Meaning of the Church*, 46–68. Grand Rapids: Eerdmans, 2011.

———. *Migrations of the Holy: God, State, and the Political Meaning of the Church*. Grand Rapids: Eerdmans, 2011.

———. *The Myth of Religious Violence: Secular Ideology and the Roots of Modern Conflict*. New York: Oxford University Press, 2009.

———. *Theopolitical Imagination*. New York: T&T Clark, 2002.

———. *Torture and Eucharist: Theology, Politics and the Body of Christ*. Oxford: Blackwell, 1998.

Clark, Victoria. *Allies for Armageddon: The Rise of Christian Zionism*. New Haven: Yale University Press, 2007.

Cohn, Norman. *The Pursuit of the Millennium*. London: Temple Smith, 1970.

Cohn-Sherbok, Dan. *The Politics of Apocalypse: The History and Influence of Christian Zionism*. London: Oneworld, 2006.

Collier, Charles. "A Nonviolent Augustinianism?: History and Politics in the Theologies of St. Augustine and John Howard Yoder." PhD diss., Duke University, 2008.

 Collins, John. *Apocalypse, Prophecy, and Pseudepigraphy: On Jewish Apocalyptic Literature*. Cambridge: Eerdmans, 2015.

Cone, James H. *Black Theology and Black Power*. Maryknoll: Orbis, 1997.

———. *The Cross and the Lynching Tree*. Maryknoll: Orbis, 2011.

———. *God of the Oppressed*. Maryknoll: Orbis, 1997.

Copeland, M. Shawn. *Enfleshing Freedom: Body, Race, and Being*. Minneapolis: Fortress, 2010.

———. "Memory, #BlackLivesMatter, and Theologians." *Political Theology* 17, no. 1 (January 2016).

D'Costa, Gavin. *Theology in the Public Square: Church, Academy and Nation*. Oxford: Blackwell, 2005.

Dula, Peter, and Chris K. Huebner, eds. *The New Yoder*. Cambridge: Lutterworth, 2011.

Eagleton, Terry. *Hope without Optimism*. New Haven: Yale University Press, 2015.

Friedman, Robert I. "The Settlers." *New York Review of Books* 36, no. 10 (June 15, 1989).

———. "West Bank Story." *New York Review of Books* 36, no. 18 (November 23, 1989).

Fulkerson, Mary McClintock. *Places of Redemption: Theology for a Worldly Church*. Oxford: Oxford University Press, 2007.

Goertz, Hans-Jürgen. *The Anabaptists*. Translated by Trevor Johnson. New York: Routledge, 1988.

Goosen, Rachel Waltner. "'Defanging the Beast': Mennonite Responses to John Howard Yoder's Sexual Abuse." *Mennonite Quarterly Review* 89, no. 1 (January 2015) 7–80.

Gregory, Eric. *Politics and the Order of Love: An Ethic of Democratic Citizenship*. Chicago: University of Chicago Press, 2008.

Gregory, Eric, and Joseph Clair, "Augustinianisms and Thomisms." In *The Cambridge Companion to Christian Political Theology*, edited by Craig Hovey and Elizabeth Phillips, 176–95. Cambridge: Cambridge University Press, 2015.

Guest, Matthew, Karin Tusting, and Linda Woodhead, eds. *Congregational Studies in the UK: Christianity in a Post-Christian Context*. Aldershot: Ashgate, 2004.

Gutierrez, Gustavo. *A Theology of Liberation*. Maryknoll: Orbis, 1988.

Hagee, John. *Beginning of the End: The Assassination of Yitzhak Rabin and the Coming Antichrist*. Nashville: Thomas Nelson, 1996.

———. *From Daniel to Doomsday: The Countdown Has Begun*. Nashville: Thomas Nelson, 1999.

———. "Why Christians Should Support Israel." *John Hagee Ministries*, January 1, 2018. https://www.jhm.org/Articles/2018-01-01-support-israel.

Hale, Charles R. "What Is Activist Research?" *Items and Issues* 2, nos. 1–2 (Summer 2001) 13–15.

Harding, Susan Friend. *The Book of Jerry Falwell: Fundamentalist Language and Politics*. Princeton: Princeton University Press, 2000.

Harink, Douglas. "The Anabaptist and the Apostle: John Howard Yoder as a Pauline Theologian." In *A Mind Patient and Untamed: Assessing John Howard Yoder's*

Contributions to Theology, Ethics, and Peacemaking, edited by Ben C. Ollenburger and Gayle Gerber Koontz, 274–87. Telford: Cascadia, 2004.

Hauerwas, Stanley. *Hannah's Child: A Theologian's Memoir.* Grand Rapids: Eerdmans, 2010.

———. "In Defence of 'Our Respectable Culture': Trying to Make Sense of John Howard Yoder's Sexual Abuse." *ABC Religion and Ethics,* October 18, 2017. http://www.abc.net.au/religion/articles/2017/10/18/4751367.htm.

———. "The Ministry of a Congregation: Rethinking Christian Ethics for a Church-Centered Seminary." In *Christian Existence Today: Essays on Church, World, and Living in Between,* 111–31. Durham: Labyrinth, 1988.

———. *The Peaceable Kingdom.* Notre Dame: University of Notre Dame Press, 1983.

Healy, Nicholas M. *Church, World and the Christian Life: Practical-Prophetic Ecclesiology.* Cambridge: Cambridge University Press, 2000.

Herman, Judith Lewis. *Trauma and Recovery: From Domestic Abuse to Political Terror.* London: Pandora, 1992.

Horowitz, Mardi. *Stress Response Syndromes.* Northvale: Jason Aronson, 1986.

Hunt, Stephen, ed. *Christian Millenarianism from the Early Church to Waco.* Bloomington: Indiana University Press, 2001.

Hütter, Reinhard L. "The Church: Midwife of History or Witness of the Eschaton?" *Journal of Religious Ethics* 18 (Spring 1990) 27–54.

Jenkins, Timothy. "The Anthropology of Christianity: Situation and Critique." *Ethnos* 77, no. 4 (2012) 459–76.

Kant, Immanuel. *Anthropology from a Pragmatic Point of View.* Translated by Robert B. Louden. Cambridge: Cambridge University Press, 2006.

———. "Of the Different Human Races." In *The Idea of Race,* edited by Robert Bernasconi and Tommy L. Lott, 8–22. Indianapolis: Hackett, 2000.

———. *Religion and Rational Theology.* Edited and translated by Allen W. Wood and George di Giovanni. Cambridge: Cambridge University Press, 1996.

Katongole, Emmanuel. *Born from Lament: The Theology and Politics of Hope in Africa.* Grand Rapids: Eerdmans, 2017.

Kirwan, Michael. *Political Theology: A New Introduction.* London: Darton, Longman and Todd, 2008.

Kolk, Bessel A. van der. "The Trauma Spectrum: The Interaction of Biological and Social Events in the Genesis of the Trauma Response." *Journal of Traumatic Stress* 1, no. 3 (January 1988) 273–90.

Krahn, Cornelius, Nanne van der Zijpp, and James Stayer. "Münster Anabaptists." In *Mennonite Encyclopedia,* edited by Cornelius J. Dyck and Dennis D. Martin, Vol. 3, 777–83, and Vol. 5, 606–7. Hillsboro: Mennonite Brethren, 1959.

Kraus, C. Norman. *Dispensationalism in America: Its Rise and Development.* Richmond: John Knox, 1958.

Lamb, Matthew L. "Wisdom Eschatology in Augustine and Aquinas." In *Aquinas the Augustinian,* edited by Michael Dauphinais, Barry David, and Matthew Levering, 258–76. Washington, DC: Catholic University of America Press, 2007.

Lazaroff, Tovah. "PM: Ariel Is the 'Capital of Samaria.'" *Jerusalem Post,* January 29, 2010.

Leget, Carlo. "Eschatology." In *The Theology of Thomas Aquinas,* edited by Rik Van Nieuwenhove and Joseph Wawrykow, 365–85. Notre Dame: University of Notre Dame Press, 2005.

LeMasters, Philip. *The Import of Eschatology in John Howard Yoder's Critique of Constantinianism.* San Francisco: Mellen Research University Press, 1992.

Lindbeck, George. *The Nature of Doctrine: Religion and Theology in a Postliberal Age.* Philadelphia: Westminster, 1984.

Lindsey, Hal, with Carole C. Carlson. *The Late Great Planet Earth.* Grand Rapids: Zondervan, 1970.

Lloyd, Vincent. "Afro-Pessimism and Christian Hope." In *Grace, Governance and Globalization,* edited by Stephan van Erp et al., 191–207. London: Bloomsbury, 2017.

Long, Duane Stephen. "Moral Theology." In *The Oxford Handbook of Systematic Theology,* 25. New York: Oxford University Press, 2007.

Luther, Martin. "Address to the Christian Nobility of the German Nationality." In *Religion and Political Thought,* edited by Michael Hoelzl and Graham Ward, 68–73. London: Continuum, 2006.

———. "On Secular Authority: How Far does the Obedience Owed to It Extend?" In *Luther and Calvin on Secular Authority,* edited and translated by Harro Höpfl, 3–43. Cambridge: Cambridge University Press, 1991.

Marsden, George. *Fundamentalism and American Culture: The Shaping of Twentieth-Century Evangelicalism: 1870–1925.* New York: Oxford University Press, 1980.

Marty, Martin E. *Righteous Empire: The Protestant Experience in America.* New York: Dial Press, 1970.

Mathewes, Charles. *A Theology of Public Life.* Cambridge: Cambridge University Press, 2007.

McBride, Jennifer. *The Church for the World: A Theology of Public Witness.* New York, NY: Oxford University Press, 2012.

McCabe, Herbert. *The Good Life.* Edited by Brian Davies. London: Bloomsbury, 2012.

———. *Law, Love and Language.* London: Sheed and Ward, 1968.

———. "The Validity of Absolutes." *Commonweal,* January 14, 1966. https://www.commonwealmagazine.org/validity-absolutes.

McClendon, James William, Jr. *Biography as Theology: How Life Stories Can Remake Today's Theology.* Philadelphia: Trinity Press International, 1990.

Mearsheimer, John J., and Stephen M. Walt. *The Israel Lobby and U.S. Foreign Policy.* New York: Farrar, Straus and Giroux, 2007.

Metz, Johannes. *Theology of the World.* Translated by William Glen-Doepel. London: Burns and Oats, 1969.

Milbank, John. *Theology and Social Theory: Beyond Secular Reason.* Oxford: Blackwell, 2006.

Moltmann, Jürgen. *Theology of Hope.* London: SCM, 1967.

Murphy, Nancey. "John Howard Yoder's Systematic Defense of Christian Pacifism." In *The Wisdom of the Cross: Essays in Honor of John Howard Yoder,* edited by Stanley Hauerwas, 168–86. Grand Rapids: Eerdmans, 1999.

Nation, Mark Theissen. *John Howard Yoder: Mennonite Patience, Evangelical Witness, Catholic Convictions.* Grand Rapids: Eerdmans, 2006.

———. "Yoder, John Howard (1927–1997)." *Global Anabaptist Mennonite Encyclopedia Online,* July 15, 2022. http://gameo.org/index.php?title=Yoder,_John_Howard_(1927-1997)&oldid=130443.

Niebuhr, Reinhold. "The Ethic of Jesus and the Social Problem." In *Love and Justice,* 29–39. Louisville: Westminster John Knox, 1957.

———. *Faith and History.* London: Nisbet and Co., 1949.

O'Connell, Maureen. "Disturbing the Aesthetics of Race." In *Enfleshing Theology: Embodiment, Discipleship, and Politics in the Work of M. Shawn Copeland*, edited by Michele Saracino and Robert J. Rivera, 233–48. Lanham: Fortress Academic, 2018.

O'Connor, Flannery. *Collected Works*. New York: Library of America, 1988.

———. *Mystery and Manners: Occasional Prose*. New York: Farrar, Straus and Giroux, 1970.

Oppenheimer, Mark. "A Theologian's Influence, and Stained Past, Live On." *New York Times*, October 12, 2013, A14.

Paraszczuk, Joanna. "Ariel Gets University Status Despite Opposition." *Jerusalem Post*, July 17, 2012.

Phillips, Elizabeth. *Political Theology: A Guide for the Perplexed*. London: T&T Clark, 2012.

Pitts, Jamie. "Anabaptist Re-Vision: On John Howard Yoder's Misrecognized Sexual Politics." *Mennonite Quarterly Review* 89, no. 1 (2015) 153–70.

———. "Liberative and Congregational: An Anabaptist Social Theory for Practical Theology." Paper delivered at the American Academy of Religion Annual Conference, Chicago, November 2, 2008.

Portier-Young, Anathea E. *Apocalypse against Empire: Theologies of Resistance in Early Judaism*. Grand Rapids: Eerdmans, 2011.

Rauschenbusch, Walter. *A Theology for the Social Gospel*. Louisville: Westminster John Knox, 1997.

Reuther, Rosemary Radford. *The Radical Kingdom: The Western Experience of Messianic Hope*. New York: Harper and Row, 1970.

Robbins, Joel. *Becoming Sinners: Christianity and Moral Torment in a Papua New Guinea Society*. Berkeley: University of California Press, 2004.

Robbins, Thomas, and Susan J. Palmer, eds. *Millennium, Messiahs, and Mayhem*. New York: Routledge, 1997.

Roth, John D., ed. *Engaging Anabaptism: Conversations with a Radical Tradition*. Scottdale: Herald, 2001.

Rutenberg, Jim, Mike McIntire, and Ethan Bronner. "Tax Exempt Funds Aid Settlements in West Bank." *New York Times*, July 5, 2010.

Salgado, Soli. "Yoder Case Extends to Notre Dame." *National Catholic Reporter*, June 19— July 2, 2015.

Sandeen, Ernest R. *The Roots of Fundamentalism: British and American Millenariansim, 1800–1930*. Grand Rapids: Baker, 1970.

Schlabach, Gerald. "The Christian Witness in the Earthly City: John Howard Yoder as Augustinian Interlocutor." In *A Mind Patient and Untamed: Assessing John Howard Yoder's Contributions to Theology, Ethics, and Peacemaking*, edited by Ben C. Ollenburger and Gayle Gerber Koontz, 221–44. Telford: Cascadia, 2004.

Schreiter, Robert. *Constructing Local Theologies*. New York: Orbis, 1985.

Scott, Peter Manley. "Kingdom Come: Introduction." In *An Eerdmans Reader in Contemporary Political Theology*, edited by William T. Cavanaugh et al., 159–64. Grand Rapids: Eerdmans, 2012.

Scott, Peter, and William T. Cavanaugh, eds. *The Blackwell Companion to Political Theology*. Oxford: Blackwell Publishing, 2007.

Scriven, Charles "The Reformation Radicals Ride Again." *Christianity Today* 34, no. 4 (1990) 13–15.

Sizer, Stephen. *Christian Zionism: Roadmap to Armageddon?* Leicester: InterVarsity, 2004.

Smith, James K.A. *Introducing Radical Orthodoxy: Mapping a Post-Secular Theology.* Grand Rapids: Baker Academic, 2004.

Smith, Ted A. *Weird John Brown: Divine Violence and the Limits of Ethics.* Stanford: Stanford University Press, 2015.

Smith, Theophus. *Conjuring Culture: Biblical Formations of Black America.* New York: Oxford University Press, 1994.

———. "Ethnography-as-Theology: Inscribing the African American Sacred Story." In *Theology Without Foundations: Religious Practice and the Future of Theological Truth,* edited by Stanley Hauerwas, Nancey Murphy, and Mark Nation, 117–39. Nashville: Abingdon, 1994.

Smith, Timothy L. *Revivalism and Social Reform: American Protestantism on the Eve of the Civil War.* New York: Harper and Row, 1957.

Stassen, Glen. *Just Peacemaking: Transforming Initiatives for Justice and Peace.* Louisville: Westminster John Knox, 1992.

———. *Just Peacemaking: Ten Practices for Abolishing War.* Cleveland: Pilgrim, 2004.

Wagner, Donald E. *Anxious for Armageddon: A Call to Partnership for Middle Eastern and Western Churches.* Scottdale: Herald, 1995.

Weber, Timothy. *Living in the Shadow of the Second Coming: American Premillennialism, 1875–1925.* New York: Oxford University Press, 1979.

———. *On the Road to Armageddon: How Evangelicals Became Israel's Best Friend.* Grand Rapids: Baker Academic, 2004.

Wells, Samuel. *Transforming Fate into Destiny: The Theological Ethics of Stanley Hauerwas.* Carlisle: Paternoster, 1998.

Wilderson, Frank D., III. *Red, White, and Black: Cinema and the Structure of U.S. Antagonisms.* Durham: Duke University Press, 2010.

Williams, Rowan. *Faith in the Public Square.* London: Bloomsbury, 2012.

———. *A Ray of Darkness: Sermons and Reflections.* Boston: Cowley, 1995.

———. *The Tragic Imagination.* Oxford: Oxford University Press, 2016.

Wilson, Dwight. *Armageddon Now! The Premillennial Response to Russia and Israel Since 1917.* Grand Rapids: Baker, 1977.

Wink, Walter. *Engaging the Powers: Discernment and Resistance in a World of Domination.* Minneapolis: Fortress, 1992.

Yoder, John Howard. "Armaments and Eschatology." *Studies in Christian Ethics* 1, no. 1 (1988) 43–61.

———. *The Christian Witness to the State.* Scottdale: Herald, 2002.

———. "Discerning the Kingdom of God in the Struggles of the World." *International Review of Missions* 68 (October 1979) 366–72.

———. "Ethics and Eschatology." *Ex Auditu* 6 (1990) 119–28.

———. *For the Nations: Essays Evangelical and Public.* Grand Rapids: Eerdmans, 1997.

———. *The Jewish–Christian Schism Revisited.* Grand Rapids: Eerdmans, 2003.

———. *Nevertheless: The Varieties and Shortcomings of Religious Pacifism.* Rev. ed. Scottdale: Herald, 1992.

———. "On Not Being in Charge." In *War and Its Discontents: Pacifism and Quietism in the Abrahamic Traditions,* edited by J. Patout Burns, 74–90. Washington, DC: Georgetown University Press, 1996.

———. "The Original Revolution." In *The Original Revolution: Essays on Christian Pacifism,* 13–33. Scottdale: Herald, 1971.

―――. "The Otherness of the Church." In *The Royal Priesthood: Essays Ecclesiastical and Ecumenical,* edited by Michael G. Cartwright, 53–64. Grand Rapids: Eerdmans, 1994.

―――. "Peace without Eschatology?" In *The Royal Priesthood: Essays Ecclesiastical and Ecumenical,* edited by Michael G. Cartwright, 153–67. Grand Rapids: Eerdmans, 1994.

―――. *The Politics of Jesus: Vicit Agnus Noster.* 2nd ed. Grand Rapids: Eerdmans, 1994.

―――. *Preface to Theology: Christology and Theological Method.* Grand Rapids: Brazos, 2002.

―――. *The Priestly Kingdom: Social Ethics as Gospel.* Notre Dame: University of Notre Dame Press, 1984.

―――. *The Royal Priesthood: Essays Ecclesiological and Ecumenical.* Grand Rapids: Eerdmans, 1994.

―――, ed. and trans. "The Schleitheim Brotherly Union." In *The Legacy of Michael Sattler,* 28–43. Scottdale: Herald, 1973.